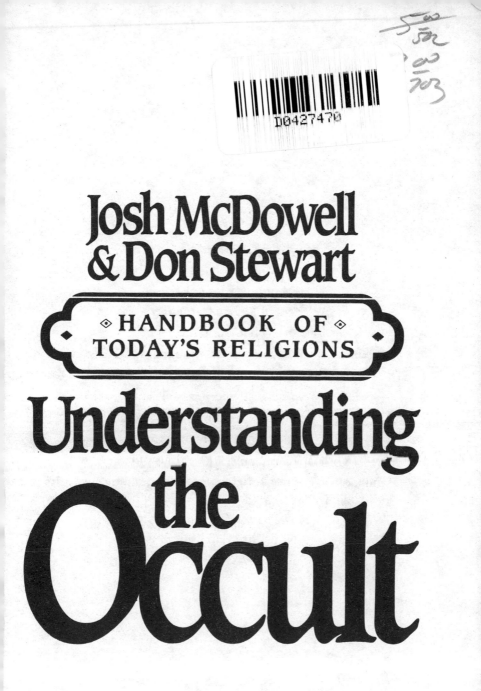

Josh McDowell & Don Stewart

◇ HANDBOOK OF ◇ TODAY'S RELIGIONS

Understanding the Occult

Understanding
the
Occult

CAMPUS CRUSADE FOR CHRIST
Published by
HERE'S LIFE PUBLISHERS, INC.
San Bernardino, California 92414

HANDBOOK OF TODAY'S RELIGIONS
Understanding the Occult
by Josh McDowell
and Don Stewart

A Campus Crusade for Christ Book

Published by
HERE'S LIFE PUBLISHERS, INC.
P. O. Box 1576
San Bernardino, CA 92402

Library of Congress Catalog Card 81-86544
ISBN 0-86605-091-4
HLP Product No. 402842
© Copyright 1982 by Campus Crusade for Christ, Inc.
All rights reserved.

Printed in the United States of America

FOR MORE INFORMATION, WRITE:

L. I. F. E. — P. O. Box A399, Sydney South 2000, Australia
Campus Crusade for Christ of Canada — Box 368, Abbottsford, B. C., V25 4N9, Canada
Campus Crusade for Christ — 103 Friar Street, Reading RGI IEP, Berkshire, England
Campus Crusade for Christ — 28 Westmoreland St., Dublin 2, Ireland
Lay Institute for Evangelism — P. O. Box 8786, Auckland 3, New Zealand
Life Ministry — P. O. Box / Bus 91015, Auckland Park 2006, Republic of So. Africa
Campus Crusade for Christ, Int'l. — Arrowhead Springs, San Bernardino, CA 92414, U.S.A.

"Beloved, believe not every spirit, but try the spirits whether they are of God, because many false prophets are gone out into the world" (1 John 4:1 KJV).

TABLE OF CONTENTS

CHAPTER ONE

The Occult Phenomena

In this book we are attempting to expose the workings of Satan and the occultic realm by the standard of God's inspired Word. In doing this, it is our desire to give a balanced picture of the situation and to avoid sensationalism. Our goals include:

(1) To be a source of information as to what is and what is not an occult phenomenon by clearing up certain misconceptions;

(2) To keep those who are not now involved in the occult from becoming so;

(3) To lead those who are now dabbling in the occult out of such practices and into a personal relationship with Jesus Christ; and

(4) To inform the believer who his real enemy is and the Satanic devices used in spiritual warfare.

What is the Occult?

The word "occult" comes from the Latin word "occultus" and it carries the idea of things hidden, secret and mysterious. Hoover lists three distinct characteristics of the occult:

1. The occult deals with things secret or hidden.
2. The occult deals with operations or events which seem to depend on human powers that go beyond the five senses.

3. The occult deals with the supernatural, the presence of angelic or demonic forces.
(David W. Hoover, *How to Respond to the Occult*, St. Louis: Concordia Publishing House, 1977, p. 8).

Under the designation occult we would class at least the following items: witchcraft, magic, palm reading, fortune telling, ouija boards, tarot cards, satanism, spiritism, demons and the use of crystal balls. To this list we could add much more.

Avoiding Extremes

C. S. Lewis once commented, "There are two equal and opposite errors into which our race can fall about the devils. One is to disbelieve in their existence. The other is to believe, and to feel an unhealthy interest in them. They themselves are equally pleased by both errors and hail a materialist or a magician with the same delight" (C. S. Lewis, *The Screwtape Letters*, New York: MacMillan Co., 1961, preface).

It is our desire to avoid such extremes that are common in dealing with the occult. We neither see the devil in everything nor completely deny his influence and workings.

Moreover, we also intend to deal with phenomena that some feel to be occultic but can be better explained either by deception, luck, or by psychological or physiological factors.

A Word of Warning

We realize that by informing people about the world of the occult, we will be exposing certain people to things and practices of which they have previously been ignorant. It is not our desire to stimulate one's curiosity in the realm of the occult to where it becomes an obsession. Seeing that mankind has a certain fascination about evil, it would be wise to take the advice of the Apostle Paul, "I want you to be wise in what is good and innocent in what is evil" (Romans 16:19, *New American Standard*).

Playing around with the world of the occult can lead to serious repercussions, both psychologically and spiritually. There is a difference between knowing intellectually that taking poison will kill you and actually taking the poison to experience what you already knew to be a fact. We need to be aware of the workings of the satanic realm but not to the point of unhealthy fascination, obsession or involvement.

The Supernatural Does Exist

We live in a day when people are looking for answers to life's basic questions, "What is the purpose of life?"; "Is there life after death?"; "Is there evidence for the existence of a supernatural God?"

In our other works we have given reasons why we believe that God exists and has revealed Himself to mankind through both the Bible and the Person of Jesus Christ.[1] This God has provided irrefutable evidence in support of the fact that He not only exists but that He is sovereign over history.

According to the Bible there is a supernatural warfare going on, "For our struggle is not against flesh and blood, but against the rulers, against the powers, against the world forces of this darkness, against the spiritual forces of wickedness in the heavenly places" (Ephesians 6:12, NASB).

This ongoing spiritual battle is between the kingdom of God and the kingdom of Satan. One purpose of Jesus Christ's coming to earth was given to us by the Apostle John, "The reason the Son of God appeared was to destroy the works of the devil" (1 John 3:8).

Although the Scriptures make it clear that the supernatural is real and that spiritual warfare is going on, there are those who would like to demythologize the accounts of the devil, demons and demon possession. They contend that the supernatural references in the Scriptures are from a pre-scientific, superstitious world view. However, if one takes the supernatural out of the Scriptures, all the meaning goes out with it. John Montgomery, dean of the Simon Greenleaf School of Law and leading contemporary theologian, comments:

[1] See *Answers to Tough Questions*, *Evidence That Demands a Verdict*, and *Reasons Skeptics Should Consider Christianity*.

Even the casual reader of the New Testament is aware of the pervasive recognition given to demonic powers. Again and again Jesus casts out demons, even engaging in dialogues with them (cf. the Gadarene demoniac incident, Luke 8); and his followers cast out demons in His name (Acts 19, etc.). Jesus' public ministry commences after He is "driven by the Spirit into the wilderness to be tempted of the devil" (Matthew 4; Mark 1; Luke 4).

Central to the entire New Testament teaching concerning the end of the world is Christ's return "with all His mighty angels," God's triumph over the evil powers, and the casting of Satan into the lake of fire forever (Matthew 25; Mark 13; 2 Thessalonians 1; Revelation 19, 20).

What is to be done with such material? One of my theological professors used to state flatly that the demonic in the New Testament was to be regarded as symbolic (of evil, psychosis, disease, etc.), and he became quite agitated when I asked him whether we should also regard Jesus as symbolic (of the good, of mental and physical health, etc.) since in the narrative of Jesus' temptation in the wilderness a dialogue takes place between Jesus and the devil—both evidently regarded as having comparable reality or unreality! This points up the difficulty with demythologizing of the satanic in the New Testament: They are integrally bound up with the reality of Jesus and His entire message. (John Warwick Montgomery, *Principalities and Powers*, Minneapolis: Bethany Fellowship, 1973, pp. 54, 55).

Those who would strip away the so-called myths from the Scripture are left with an empty gospel, devoid of any life-transforming power. In answer to such critics, we respond with the truth and rational claims of the whole gospel—including Satan's war against it and God's supernatural intervention and ultimate triumph. The world of the occult is real, and God's all-powerful Spirit is just as real!

Occultic Deception

Although we admit the reality of the supernatural, we must be careful not to place all unexplained phenomena into the supernatural category. There is much that goes on under the guise of the supernatural that is nothing but fakery. This pseudo-occult phenomenon has fooled many people into believing in its legitimacy.

In an excellent book entitled *The Fakers*, Danny Korem

and Paul Meier expose much of this phenomenon that is taken to be supernatural. They explain the difference between what is real and what is actually deception:

> What is the difference between occult and pseudo-occult phenomena? Occult phenomena are phenomena of or relating to supernatural agencies, their effects, and knowledge of them. An example which many people consider a manifestation of occultic powers is demon possession. While the manifestation is visible, the force behind it is not. We can see the *effects* of a possession, but we cannot see the demon perpetrating the manifestation. Pseudo-occult phenomena are events which *appear* to be caused by secretive, supernatural powers and yet are brought about by physical or psychological means.
>
> One purpose of this book is to point out the difference between the occult and pseudo-occult. There is a great danger in treating both on equal ground. One man who had reportedly performed the act of exorcism on several demon-possessed individuals tried his hand on a young teenager. The man strapped the young lady to a chair to prevent her from harming herself and proceeded with his ritual. It turned out that the girl was not demon-possessed but was schizophrenic and needed the help of a trained psychiatrist. The girl, obviously terrified by the trauma, was left in worse shape than when she first went to see the man in question.
>
> Misconceptions about the supernatural are legion, and it makes no difference whether one does or does not profess religious beliefs. Neither is one's level of mental competence or educational background a factor. In order for one to make qualified decisions as to whether an event is of the supernatural or not, it is helpful if one is schooled in the art of deception (Danny Korem and Paul Meier, *The Fakers*, Grand Rapids, MI: Baker Book House, 1980, pp. 15, 16).

Korem and Meier list 11 principles of deception that fakers use to imitate supernatural or occultic phenomena. These include:

1. Sleight of hand
2. Psychological principles
3. Using a stooge
4. Unseen and unknown devices
5. Mathematical principles
6. Physics
7. Physical deception
8. Mechanical deception

9. Optical illusion
10. Luck and probability
11. Combination of all the principles.
(Ibid., pp. 22-29).

Needless to say, caution must be exercised before assuming some unexplained phenomenon is demonic. While not all Christian writers would place certain phenomena under the category of deception, as Korem and Meier, the latter clearly demonstrate the need for restraint in attributing many unexplained phenomena to the occult.

What Kind of People Get Involved in the Occult?

Who gets involved in the occult and why they get involved is very important. (It is also important to remember that when we refer to the "occult," we do not mean one homogenous organization or religion. The "occult" refers to a collection of practices and beliefs generally associated with occultic phenomena. One could be in the "occult" whether he is involved in a particular occultic group or just involved with occultic practices and/or beliefs.

It is wrong to classify all occultists as either sick or on the fringe of society, for responsible professional people are practicing the occult. W. Elwyn Davies lists three characteristics which may be true of occult practitioners:

1. *Many are escapists.* It has become a cliche to say, "Satan (or the demons) made me do it." The world of the occult becomes attractive to people who find it difficult to face up to their moral responsibilities. Many dabble with "other powers," and are drawn into involvement. They often claim that they have tried "other remedies" in vain, and the alternative empowerment through the occult allures them.

2. *Many more are superstitious.* Going beyond the bounds of revelation and common sense, they profess to see demonic activity in many areas: Sickness, depression, anger, any unusual or unexplained behavior. While such may be evidence of demonic action, it should by no means be an automatic assumption. Where natural causes offer a reasonable explanation it is wise to accept them as the origin of the problem. People who jump to the conclusion

that demonic influences are responsible for a wide variety of phenomena invariably become obsessed with the thought of demons-at-work, and suffer many of the disabilities commonly found in victims of demonization.

3. *All are victims.* I use the word advisedly. There is no point in being judgmental toward these people, even though as Christians we oppose and condemn all occult practices. From a biblical perspective there is no room for negotiation or compromise here. God judges and condemns all traffic with demons, and we can do no less. In the sight of God they are guilty of transgressing His law. Each one is a victim, too—the victim of powers immeasurably more powerful and knowing than he. What kind of person is he?

   (1) The curious, who experiments and plays with demonic forces, only to find eventually that they are playing with him.

   (2) The conformist, who looks around at this peer group and says, "Everyone does it," and decides to be another who "does it."

   (3) The dissatisfied, whose religious experience has left him unfulfilled and skeptical.

   (4) The sad, whose bereavement inclines him toward anything that offers knowledge of the dead.

   (5) The rebellious, who recoils from the status quo in the church and in society, and seeks a viable alternative elsewhere.

   (6) The psychically inclined, who wants to develop suspected latent powers.

   (7) The offspring of practicing occultists, who are conditioned from childhood.

   (8) The credulous, and every generation seems to produce its quota of them! (W. Elwyn Davies, in *Principalities and Powers*, edited by John Warwick Montgomery, Minneapolis, MN: Bethany Fellowship, 1976, pp. 303, 304).

CHAPTER TWO

The Occult Explosion

We live in a day when occult activity is rapidly increasing. The following news release reveals the widespread purchase of occultic paraphernalia, along with the modern, sophisticated methods by which it is marketed:

...1980 saw another increase in occult activity in America as reflected in the marketing sophistication of occult movements.

According to Craig A. Huey, president of Informat, Inc., a Rolling Hills Estates, California-based direct marketing agency, many companies prospered greatly by marketing occult books, magazines, charms, voodoo pendants and other assorted paraphernalia. The available mailing lists involved in the occult now stands at some 3,824,622 (some include the accumulation of several years). Women still constitute a majority of the buyers. The vast majority of occultists are involved in astrology. For example, one company called the American Astrological Association has some 339,660 individuals who have bought horoscopes for an average sale of between $3.50-$9.95. There are some 86,000 women mail order buyers who paid $8.40 each for a genie-in-the-bottle good luck pendant, a mystical talisman.

The House of Collinwood has 92,976 buyers who purchased ankhs, pyramids, talisman amulets, zodiac medallions, occult necklaces, bracelets, rings, earrings, (mostly for women) at $12 apiece on the average.

There were 208,302 buyers of the *Handbook of Supernatural Powers*, which gives directions for ancient spells and potions. Seventy percent are men, and they paid $10 each. There were 91,846 buyers of the book *Magic Power of Witchcraft* at $9.98. There are 16,842 members of the Circle of Mystic and Occult Arts Book Club of Prentice Hall Publishing.

Martin Ebon, former administrative secretary of the Parapsychology Foundation, and the author of *The Satan Trap* and *Dangers of the Occult*, gives his assessment of the upswing of interest in occult phenomena:

Occult practices and psychic phenomena are exercising a hold on millions of Americans today. There is no single explanation for this boom, but its major causes are easy to pinpoint. To begin with, the age-old pull of the irrational remains as persistent and just about as inexplicable as, let's say, terrestrial gravity; and while traditional religious practices lose their attraction, the occult and related Eastern mysticism gain in popularity.

Two mass stimuli have contributed to this trend. One is the drug cult, which causes an interest in such matters as a "non-drug high," to be sought in meditation and similar practices, as well as in confirmation of the drug-induced feeling that mind may control matter or events. Second, a series of highly popular motion pictures created successive waves of occult or pseudo-occult involvements. With *Rosemary's Baby*, which pictured the birth of a diabolic infant, came an upswing in witchcraft practices; with *The Exorcist*, demonic possession and exorcism were dramatized to a public of millions; other films and television shows have dealt with similar themes.

These waves of interest, compounded, have indirectly drawn attention to scholarly research of parapsychology— although researchers in the field deplore the sensationalism that powers public interest. The mass-circulation tabloids, in particular the *National Enquirer*, bring a weekly potion of the magical and psychic to the check-out counters of the nation's supermarkets; stories of miraculous healings, haunted houses, visits by Unidentified Flying Objects, and exorcism abound in these periodicals. The very fact that these shrewdly edited publications find it profitable to mix the occult with jet-set gossip and anecdotes of awe and uplift illustrates public fascination with psychic subjects. Astrology, although in a category by itself, has a similar hold on a large public. ("The Occult Temptation," by Martin Ebon, *The Humanist*, January/February, 1977).

From the above it is evident that occult beliefs have now penetrated every web of our society (cf. The Gallup Poll: 1978, June 15; "Astrology and Marginality," *Journal for the Scientific Study of Religion*, 15: 157-169, by R. Wuthrow, 1976). From the media to grocery stores, one cannot turn without encountering some type of occultic literature or influence. One can find horoscopes for weight loss and horoscopes for a better sex life.

Even higher education is not exempt. The University of California at Berkeley recently awarded its first bachelor's degree in magic, and is only one of many reputable universities now offering courses in parapsychology.

Parapsychology is an attempt to give certain occultic practices scientific respectability. This often means assenting to their reality (such as mental telepathy, telekinesis) yet having no explanation for their source, or the means by which they operate.

Here is a description by someone sympathetic to the occult explosion:

The occult is no longer what it used to be. Only a few years ago, especially around the time of the Satanic film *Rosemary's Baby*, the term "occult" would have been reserved for obscure, demonic and vaguely diabolical practices alone. In San Francisco at this time Anton Szandor La Vey, who starred as the devil in the above film, was establishing his Satanic Church; Charles Manson was incarnating the Devil and Christ simultaneously; Bishop Pike was endeavouring to communicate with his suicide son through a medium; and witchcraft was thriving.

These days, we believe, the occult has a wider connotation. *The Exorcist* notwithstanding, the term "occult" today includes ESP, Kirlian photography, reincarnation, palmistry, astrology, faith healing, white magic, Tarot, and even out-of-the-body experiences. The occult, too, is no longer disreputable. Scientists at Stanford investigate psychic Uri Geller; in California, Professor Charles Tart carries out laboratory tests on Robert Monroe, a subject who can astral-travel at will; Arthyr Koestler, previously doubtful about the powers of yogis, comes forth with a scientific rationale of the paranormal in his *Roots of Coincidence*; Colin Wilson, meanwhile coins the term "Faculty X" to describe the psychic potential of man which he believes marks the next phase of man's evolution.

In short, the occult is about man's hidden potential. Much of this, of course, relates to how he thinks and how he perceives. Many aspects of the occult dealt with in this book show how man can enlarge his consciousness (Nevill Drury and Gregory Tillett, *The Occult Sourcebook*, London: Routledge and Kegan Paul, 1978, p. ix).

Why is There Such an Interest in the Occult?

With the alarming rate at which people are becoming involved in the occult, the inevitable question of "why" comes up, Why do people who live in this enlightened age with all the marvelous scientific and technological advances become involved in occultic practices? We believe there are several factors that have contributed to the rise of occult popularity.

The Secularization of the Gospel

In recent years there has been a denial of the cardinal doctrines of the Christian faith from those occupying a position of leadership in the church. This leaves a greater spiritual vacuum in the world which invites people who have spiritual needs to go elsewhere to have them satisfied. Moreover, some of these church leaders who have forsaken the gospel have themselves become practitioners of the occult, causing a follow-the-leader mentality in many former churchgoers.

The classic example would be the Episcopal bishop, James Pike, who rejected the church's belief in the deity of Christ, His virgin birth, and other central truths. After the suicide death of his son, Pike began to consult mediums, including the famous Arthur Ford, in an attempt to contact the spirit of his dead son. Pike became a firm believer in life after death from his occultic involvement rather than from biblical doctrine and took many people with him into the dark world of the occult. When the church "waters down" the gospel of Christ, the door to occultic practice swings wide open.

Curiosity

There is a certain mystery about the occult which appeals to our curiosity. Many who get involved in occult practices do so by starting out with so-called "harmless" practices such as reading horoscopes or using a Ouija board. They afterward proceed into deeper involvement because of an increasing curiosity. Buzzard comments upon this fascination:

> Our age seems to have a deep fascination with evil, the bizarre, and the inexplicable. It thrives on horror and repulsion. What makes one faint or vomit or experience nightmares has a kind of magnetic charm. Mary Knoblauch summed up this fascination in commenting on *The Exorcist:* "Perhaps the most frightening thing about *The Exorcist* is that thirst for and fascination with evil that lies buried in us all, surfacing with savage swiftness at the right incarnation." The moment of that incarnation seems to be upon us. What was buried has arisen and dances unashamedly in the streets (Lynn Buzzard, Introduction to *Demon Possession*, edited by John Warwick Montgomery, Minneapolis: Bethany Fellowship, 1976, pp. 17, 18).

Unfortunately, there is a price to pay for this curiosity about the occult. The occult is not something neutral that an individual can get in and out of without any adverse effects.

In his book *Kingdom of Darkness*, F. W. Thomas relates a story of a man-and-wife journalistic team who desired to investigate the occult in London. They joined a satanic group to obtain firsthand information, but eventually withdrew because of the frightening things which they observed. Their lives were never the same. They were troubled by many terrible experiences and incidents.

Thomas concluded, "Such was the experience of an unwise couple whose curiosity for black magic dragged them through untold anguish and despair. One cannot just pick up the dark bolts of magical fire and drop them at will without getting burned. There is always a price to pay for use of these forbidden powers, in this world as well as in the world to come" (F. W. Thomas, *Kingdom of Darkness*, cited by Clifford Wilson and John Weldon, *Occult Shock and Psychic Forces*, San Diego: Master Books, 1980, pp. 13, 14).

The Occult Offers Reality

There is a reality in the occultic experience which attracts many people to it. All of us desire some sort of ultimate answer for life's basic questions, and the world of the occult gladly supplies answers. The astrologist will chart your future. The Ouija board promises you direction, and the medium talking to the spirit of your dead relative informs you that things are fine in the next world.

Since these occultic practices do reveal some amazing things, the practitioner is lulled into thinking that he has experienced ultimate reality and no longer needs to continue his search for truth. The spiritual vacuum is filled by means of a spiritual experience, not with God, but often from the very pit of hell.

A Sign of the Times

There are many indications that we are living at the end of the age with the return of Jesus Christ on the horizon. If this is the case, then we should expect to see an increase in demonic activity as Christ's coming nears, for this is the clear teaching of Scripture: "But the Spirit explicitly says that in later times some will fall away from the faith, paying attention to deceitful spirits and doctrines of demons" (1 Timothy 4:1, NASB).

Jesus said that at the end of the age, "False Christs and false prophets will arise, and will show signs and wonders, in order, if possible, to lead the elect astray" (Mark 13:22, NASB). Thus, Scripture indicates that occultic activity would be on the rise shortly before the second coming of Jesus Christ.

The Bible and the Occult

The Bible categorically denounces any and all occultic practices:

> When you enter the land which the Lord your God gives you, you shall not learn to imitate the detestable things of those nations.
> There shall not be found among you anyone who makes his son or his daughter pass through the fire, one who uses divination, one who practices witchcraft, or one who interprets omens, or a sorcerer,
> or one who casts a spell, or a medium, or a spiritualist, or one who calls upon the dead.
> For whoever does these things is detestable to the Lord; and because of these detestable things the Lord your God will drive them out before you.

You shall be blameless before the Lord your God.

For those nations, which you shall dispossess, listen to those who practice witchcraft and to diviners, but as for you, the Lord your God has not allowed you to do so (Deuteronomy 18:9-14, NASB).

In the same manner, the New Testament condemns such workings (Galatians 5:20). In the city of Ephesus many who were practicing in the occult became believers in Jesus Christ and renounced their occultic practices. "Many also of those who practiced magic brought their books together and began burning them in the sight of all..." (Acts 19:19).

Another encounter with the occult can be seen in Acts 13:6-12: (NASB):

And when they had gone through the whole island as far as Paphos, they found a certain magician, a Jewish false prophet whose name was Bar-Jesus,

Who was with the proconsul, Sergius Paulus, a man of intelligence. This man summoned Barnabas and Saul and sought to hear the word of God.

But Elymas the magician (for thus his name is translated) was opposing them, seeking to turn the proconsul away from the faith.

But Saul, who was also known as Paul, filled with the Holy Spirit, fixed his gaze upon him.

And said, "You who are full of all deceit and fraud, you son of the devil, you enemy of all righteousness, will you not cease to make crooked the straight ways of the Lord?

And now, behold, the hand of the Lord is upon you, and you will be blind and not see the sun for a time. And immediately a mist and a darkness fell upon him, and he went about seeking those who would lead him by the hand.

Then the proconsul believed when he saw what happened, being amazed at the teaching of the Lord.

The false prophet who called himself Bar-Jesus (Son of Jesus) was actually trying to keep the governor, Sergius Paulus, from becoming a believer, and the judgment of blindness on this man was immediate. Walter Martin makes some astute observations on the passage by listing five characteristics of those who oppose God:

1. They are in league with Satan and possess certain supernatural powers.
2. They are false prophets.

3. They seek to influence people politically and ecclesiastically, particularly those in positions of power (verses 6, 7).

4. They attempt to prevent those who are seeking to hear the Word of God from learning it by opposing those who preach it (verse 8).

5. They deliberately attempt to divert prospective converts from the faith (verse 8) as their ultimate goal (Walter Martin, *The Maze of Mormonism*, Santa Ana, CA: Vision House Publishers, Inc., 1977, pp. 216, 217).

From the above, to which much could be added, we see how the Bible in the strongest terms condemns the occult and those who practice it. The road of the occult is broad and leads to destruction, while the way of Christ is narrow and leads to life eternal.

CHAPTER THREE

Astrology

Two of the most crucial questions that haunt humanity are, "Who am I?" and "What's going to happen in the future?" Many people lose sleep at night worrying about the future, wondering what will happen tomorrow. Astrology claims to have the solution to these basic questions. They offer daily horoscopes to predict individuals' futures. "What's your sign?" crops up in many casual conversations. The ancient occultic art of astrology has become very popular in our 20th-century culture.

What Is Astrology?

Astrology is an ancient practice that assumes that the position of the stars and planets has a direct influence upon people and events. Supposedly, one's life pattern can be charted by determining the position of the stars and planets at the time of one's birth. The chart that attempts to accomplish this is known as a "horoscope." Rene Noorbergen explains how one's horoscope is charted:

> For every personal horoscope, the moment of birth is the essential starting point. This, coupled with the latitude and longitude of the individual's birthplace, provides the initial package for the usual astrological chart. While this is elementary, it is not complete; a factor known as "true local time" must also be considered. This "true" time is arrived at by adding or subtracting four minutes for each degree of longitude that your birthplace lies to the east or west of the

center of your time zone of birth. Once this has been accomplished, the next step is to convert this "true" time into "sidereal" or star time. This is done with the aid of an ephemerus, a reference book showing the positions of the planets in relationship to the earth. Checking this star time in an astrological table is the last formal move, for in doing so, the theme of the individual's "ascendant"—the astrological sign that is supposed to have been rising on the eastern horizon at the moment of birth—is revealed.

Once you have developed this data—these simple steps are no more difficult than solving a seventh-grade math problem—then you are ready to "chart" your horoscope. This means you align the "ascendant" with the nine-o'clock point on the inner circle of the horoscope, and from there you are prepared to "read" the various zodiacal "houses" that control your life and fortune (Rene Noorbergen, *The Soul Hustlers*, Grand Rapids, MI: Zondervan, 1976, pp. 176, 177).

How Is It Justified?

How astrologers justify their practice is explained by Michael Van Buskirk:

> One's future can be forecast, allegedly, because astrology asserts the unity of all things. This is the belief that the Whole (or all of the universe put together) is in some way the same as the Part (or the individual component or man), or that the Part is a smaller reflection of the Whole (macro-cosmic/microcosmic model). The position of the planets (the macro) influences and produces a corresponding reaction in man (the micro). This makes man a pawn in the cosmos with his life and actions pre-determined and unalterable (Michael Van Buskirk, *Astrology: Revival in the Cosmic Garden*, Costa Mesa, CA: Caris, 1976, p. 6)

Noorbergen concludes, "To believe in astrology, you must support the philosophy that you are either a 'born loser' or a 'born winner.' The stars, we are being told, do not merely forecast the course of our lives, but they also cause the events to take place. They both impel and compel..." (Rene Noorbergen, op. cit., pp. 178, 179).

The Problems of Astrology

The claims that astrologists have made have drawn severe criticism from the scientific community. In September, 1975, 186 prominent American scientists, along with 18 Nobel Prize winners, spoke out against "the pretentious claims of astrological charlatans," saying, among other things, that there is no scientific basis whatsoever for the assumption that the stars foretell events and influence lives. The following are some of the reasons the practice of astrology must be rejected as both unscientific and unbiblical.

The Problem of Authority

Astrologists are victims of their own system. They cannot have the objective authority necessary to explain our own world. If everything is predetermined in conjunction with the zodiac, then how can the astrologists get outside of that fatalism to accurately observe it?

What if the astrologists themselves are predetermined to explain everything by astrology? There is no way they can prove their system if they are pawns in that same system. By contrast, as Christians we can test our own world view because someone, Jesus Christ, has come from outside the "system" to tell us, objectively, what our system is like.

Conflicting Systems

The problem of authority in astrology is graphically revealed when one realizes there are many systems of astrology which are diametrically opposed to each other. Astrologers in the West would not interpret a horoscope the same way a Chinese astrologer would.

Even in the West, there is no unanimity of interpretation among astrologers, seeing that some contend for eight zodiac signs rather than 12, while others argue for 14 or even 24 signs of the zodiac.

With these different systems employed by astrologers, an individual may go to two different astrologers and receive two totally opposed courses of behavior for the same day! This is not only a possibility, it is also a reality, for a simple comparison between astrological forecasts in daily newspapers will often reveal contradictions.

Earth Centered Viewpoint

Astrology is based upon the premise that the planets revolve around the earth, known as the "geocentric theory." This theory was shown to be in error by Copernicus, who proved that the planets revolve around the sun, not the earth. This is known as the "heliocentric theory."

Since astrology is based upon the refuted geocentric theory, its reliability is destroyed. Since the basic assumption is false, all conclusions, even if feebly reinterpreted by today's knowledge and drawn from this assumption, are likewise false.

Missing Planets

One of the major misconceptions that is the basis of astrology concerns the number of planets in our solar system. Most astrological charts are based upon the assumption that there are seven planets in our solar system (including the sun and the moon).

In ancient times, Uranus, Neptune and Pluto were unobservable with the naked eye. Consequently, astrologers based their system upon the seven planets they believed revolved around the earth. Since that time, it has been proven that the sun, not the earth, is the center of the solar system and that three other planets exist in our solar system.

According to the astrological theory, that the position of planets has a definite influence upon human behavior and events, these three previously undiscovered planets should also have an influence upon behavior and must be considered to cast an exact horoscope. Since they usually are not considered, the astrological theory breaks down, for no accurate horoscope could be charted without considering all the planets and their supposed influence.

Twins

A constant source of embarrassment for astrologers is the birth of twins. Since they are born at exactly the same time and place, they should have the same destiny. Unfortunately, this is not the case, for experience shows us that two people who are born at the same time can live totally different lives. One may turn out to be very successful, while the other ends up a failure. The fact that twins do not live out the same lives shows another flaw in the theory.

Limited Perspective

A serious problem with astrology is its limited perspective. Astrology was born in an area close to the equator and did not take into consideration those living in latitudes where the zodiac signs do not appear for the same periods of time.

As Michel Gauquelin points out, "Astrology, begun in latitudes relatively close to the equator, made no provisions for the possibility that no planet may be in sight (in the higher latitudes) for several weeks in a row" (Michel Gauquelin, *The Cosmic Clocks*, Chicago, IL: Henry Regnery Co., 1967, p. 78).

This means those living in the higher latitudes in places such as Alaska, Norway, Finland and Greenland have no planetary influence in their lives, for it is almost impossible to calculate what point of the zodiac is rising on the horizon above the Arctic circle.

Since this is the case, one of the basic pillars of astrology now crumbles, as Van Buskirk points out, "Astrology can hardly be scientifically based on its own premise that the microcosm reflects the influence of the macrocosm, when one of the microcosms (man) above the 66th latitude is left uninfluenced by the cosmos" (Michael Van Buskirk, op. cit., p. 9).

No Scientific Verification

Probably the most damaging criticism that can be leveled at astrological prediction is the fact that its scientific value is nil. Paul Couderc, astronomer at the Paris Observatory, concluded after examining the horoscopes of 2,817 musicians:

> The position of the sun has absolutely no musical significance. The musicians are born throughout the entire year on a chance basis. No sign of the zodiac or fraction of a sign favors or does not favor them.
>
> We conclude: The assets of scientific astrology are equal to zero, as is the case with commercialized astrology. This is perhaps unfortunate, but it is a fact (Paul Couderc, *L'Astrologie*, "Que Sais-je?" 508; 3rd ed.; Paris: Presses Universitaires de France, 1961, pp. 86-89, cited by John Warwick Montgomery, *Principalities and Powers*, p. 106).

The statistics to support the predictive claims of astrologers are simply not there.

Incorrect Time of Reckoning

Another major problem with astrology concerns the fact that horoscopes are cast from the time of birth, not from the time of conception. Since all the hereditary factors are determined at conception, it should logically follow that the planets could begin influencing the person's destiny immediately after conception.

The problem is, of course, trying to accurately determine when conception took place, which is nearly impossible. However, if the planets do exert an influence over a person's fate, it should start at the time of conception rather than the time of birth.

The Shifting Constellations

Astrology is unscientific because of the fact of the precession or the shifting of constellations. Boa elaborates on this problem:

> The early astronomers were not aware of precession and therefore failed to take it into account in their system. The twelve signs of the zodiac originally correspond with the twelve constellations of the same names. But due to precession, the constellations have shifted about 30° in the last 2,000 years. This means that the constellation of Virgo is now in the sign of Libra, the constellation of Libra is now in the sign of Scorpio and so on. Thus, if a person is born on September 1, astrologers would call him a Virgo (the sign the sun is in at that date), but the sun is actually in the constellation Leo at that date. So there are two different zodiacs: one which slowly moves (the sidereal zodiac) and one which is stationary (the tropical zodiac). Which zodiac should be used? (Kenneth Boa, *Cults, World Religions, and You*, Victor Books, 1977, pp. 124, 125).

Furthermore, no constellation *ever* recurs. As Koch points out, "The most weighty factor is the astronomer's objection that no constellation in the sky ever recurs. Hence, astrological interpretations lack every basis of comparison. Hence, solstitial horoscopy rests on presuppositions which are scientifically untenable" (Kurt Koch, *Christian Counseling and Occultism*, Grand Rapids: Kregel Pub., 1973, p. 94).

The Bible and Astrology

The Bible warns people against relying on astrologers and astrology:

> You are wearied with your many counsels; let now the astrologers, those who prophesy by the stars, those who predict by the new moons, stand up and save you from what will come upon you. Behold, they have become like stubble, fire burns them; they cannot deliver themselves from the power of the flame...there is none to save you (Isaiah 47: 13-15, NASB).

Other warnings can be found in such verses as Jeremiah 10:2: "Learn not the way of the heathen, and be not dismayed at the signs of Heaven; for the heathen are dismayed at them." Elsewhere, the Scripture says, "And beware, lest you lift up your eyes to heaven and see the sun and the moon and the stars, all the host of heaven, and be drawn away and worship them and serve them" (Deuteronomy 4:19, NASB).

The Book of Daniel gives us a comparison between the astologers and those dedicated to the true and living God. Chapter 1:20 reveals that Daniel and his three friends would be ten times better in matters of wisdom and understanding than the astrologers because they served the living and true God rather than the stars. When the king had a dream, the astrologers could not give an explanation for it, but rather God alone had the answer, for it is only He who can reveal the future (see Daniel 2: 27, 28).

The Scriptures make it clear that any type of astrological practice is severely condemned by God, for it attempts to understand the future through occultic means rather than through God's divinely inspired Word. The fatalistic approach of astrology, which says our lives are determined by the stars, is contradicted by Scripture, which holds us responsible for our destiny. Astrology and Christianity are simply incompatible.

Dangers of Astrology

There are some very real dangers in trying to live your life by a horoscope.

First is the attempt to try to run your life by following along in astrology. Since it is apparent a great deal of astrology has no basis in reality, you run the risk of great loss.

There can be the loss of money, both of what you may spend on astrology and what the astrologers may recommend for you to do. They may recommend you invest now, buy later, don't purchase this, etc. These recommended investments are no more certain than a fortune cookie, and you could suffer considerable financial loss.

Second, a person who continually tries to live his life by a horoscope can become very depressed as he begins to see life as fatalistic, predetermined since his birth, with no opportunity to break free. Women have even refused the medical advice of induced labor for a late pregnancy in order to have their baby born later, so as to be an Aquarius, for example.

> There is something pitiable about a lady I know who resides in a part of Europe not known for sophisticated medical practices and who refused to have the two-and-a-half-week-late birth of her child induced because she wanted him to be an Aquarius instead of whatever comes before that. I hope that the child suffers no unfortunate consequences (Samuel Hux, *The Humanist*, May/June 1978, "Parawhatsit: A Certain Incapacity to Appreciate the World," p. 32).

Numerology

Numerology is a close cousin of astrology. It too involves such aspects as a person's birth and the use of the planets. Dennis Wheatley states of numerology:

> This is closely allied to astrology and is said to have its origins in the learning of the ancient Hindus. Their priesthood was sufficiently far advanced in the science of astronomy to be aware of the precession of the equinoxes, which is completed once every 25,827 years; so one cannot lightly dismiss their belief in astrology and the potency of numbers. The belief they held was that each heavenly body is associated with a number, which partakes of its qualities.
>
> The date of a person's birth automatically associates him with one number, but that produced by substituting the above numbers for the letters of his name is considered even more important. Should the two be the same, that obviously greatly increases the influence of the planet associated with that number and adds to the potency gained when a person uses that number to further his projects (Dennis Wheatley,

The Devil and All His Works, NY: American Heritage Press, 1971, p. 46).

Why do People Believe in Astrology?

If astrology is both unscientific and unbiblical, why do so many people believe in it?

One answer would be that it sometimes works, as one book on astrology attests: "When the late astrological genius, Grant Lewi, was asked why he believed in astrology, his blunt answer was, 'I believe in it because it works.' This is as good an answer as any...we say that astrology works because it is based on natural law" (Joseph Polansky, *Sun Sign Success*, New York: Warner/Destiny Books, 1977, p. 35).

There is a much better explanation for the so-called accuracy of astrological predictions. If one reads a horoscope, even in a cursory manner, he will be struck with the general and ambiguous nature of the statements, which can be pointed to as fulfilling anything and everything. *Time Magazine* observed:

> There are so many variables and options to play with that the astrologer is always right. Break a leg when your astrologer told you the signs were good, and he can congratulate you on escaping what might have happened had the signs been bad. Conversely, if you go against the signs and nothing happens, the astrologer can insist that you were subconsciously careful because you were forewarned (*Time Magazine*, March 21, 1969, p. 56).

The suggestive aspect also needs to be taken into consideration, as Koch has pointed out: "The person who seeks advice from an astrologer comes with a certain readiness to believe the horoscope. This predisposition leads to an autosuggestion to order his life according to the horoscope, and thus contribute to its fulfillment" (Kurt Koch, *Occult and Christian Counseling*, op. cit., p. 95).

Wilson and Weldon illustrate this point:

> Rachleff tells of a very interesting experiment in which an identical horoscope was mailed to over 100 persons who had given their natal information to a post office box number. The recipients had 12 different birth periods represented by their birth dates, and their varieties were as opposite as could be expected, through Leo and Cancer. Each person was told

that the horoscope sent out pertained only to that one person, and basically they accepted it as such. He tells us that "many admired its pertinence and exactitude" (p. 38). The fact is, if enough information is given, we are able to find ways in which it fits our own experiences (Clifford Wilson and John Weldon, *Occult Shock and Psychic Forces*, San Diego: Master Books, 1980, p. 118).

Astrology is bankrupt both biblically and scientifically. Since it is fatalistic in its approach, it rules out the free choice of each of us, leaving man merely as a cog in the cosmic machinery. This view of reality is at odds with Scripture, which indicates all of us have both the capacity and responsibility to choose which road in life we will take.

Astrology would deny us that choice and therefore must be rejected. The Scriptures show us a better way of looking into the future, seeing that God has already told us what the future holds for each of us and for our planet.

CHAPTER FOUR

The Black Mass

The black mass is said in honor of the devil at the witches' Sabbath. It is practiced by many satanic groups. The ritual reverses the Roman Catholic mass, desecrating the objects used in worship. Oftentimes a nude woman is stretched out upon the altar where the high priest ends the ritual by having sex with her.

Sometimes the participants drink the blood of an animal during the ceremony, along with the eating of human flesh in a mock communion ritual. Human sacrifices, though rare, are not unknown to the black mass.

The black mass contains many other repulsive practices that are unmentionable. It perverts and desecrates the true worship of God and is a blasphemous affront to all believers in Christ.

Clifford Wilson and John Weldon described a black mass as follows:

> Normally, a small group of people sit in front of a table covered with a purple velvet altar cloth, lit with candles. Over the "altar" hangs a cross upside down and a picture of the devil, half-human, half-beast. A high priest stands by the table dressed in bishop's robes. On his person he wears an inverted cross. He throws a larger cross to the floor. "Shemhaforash," he shouts. This is probably the most powerful word uttered in satanic worship. According to the Talmud (a book of Jewish civil and religious laws and ethical lore) it was the secret mystic word spoken by God when He

created the world. He then spits upon the cross, with an obscene gesture, and cries, "Hail Satan!" Thus begins the sickening and blasphemous ritual, as the devil worshippers repeat the Lord's prayer backwards and make mockery of the ordinances of the church. One quotation from LaVey's "The Satanic Bible" says, "Blessed are the strong, for they shall possess the earth." "If a man smite you on one cheek, smash him on the other!"

Nudity is commonly found at satanic covens. When a witch is initiated, she is symbolically "sacrificed" to the sun god, and this ceremony takes place while she is lying naked on the altar. The power of the witch is said to be heightened by the mysterious force that is within her own body, and when clothing is worn that power is supposedly obstructed. Their delusion is that they will gain pleasure and enjoyment in this world, especially of a sensual nature and that in a coming age Satan will overcome the Christians' God and return to the heaven from which he was once thrown out. Satan's earthly followers, so the delusion goes, will then share fruits of eternal power with his spirit forces (Clifford Wilson and John Weldon, *Occult Shock and Psychic Forces*, San Diego: Master Books, 1980, pp. 9, 10).

The black mass is today's perfect image of the occultism so clearly condemned by the Lord in the Old and New Testaments. It is not possible to serve Satan and Jesus Christ. Christians should have nothing to do with the black mass or any satanic or witchcraft practices. They are perversions of the true Gospel. As perversions, they bring eternal death rather than the eternal life promised by Jesus Christ.

A day will come when even Satan, his demons and those who are bound in the occult will no longer celebrate the black mass, but will be forced to bow to the Lord Jesus Christ. "At the name of Jesus every knee should bow, of those who are in heaven, and on earth, and under the earth, and that every tongue should confess that Jesus Christ is Lord, to the glory of God the Father" (Philippians 2:10, 11, NASB).

CHAPTER FIVE

Edgar Cayce and the A.R.E.

A man who has caused considerable controversy in the 20th century with his prophetic utterings was Edgar Cayce, known as the "sleeping prophet" because of the prophecies he gave while he appeared to be sleeping.

Born in Kentucky in 1877, Cayce realized at an early age that he was clairvoyant and he was determined to use his gift for the betterment of mankind. At the age of 21 Cayce was struck with paralysis of the throat, losing most of his ability to speak. After some time Cayce diagnosed his disease and prescribed a cure while in a self-induced trance. The word quickly spread of the strange ability he possessed.

Cayce began to diagnose illnesses and prescribe cures for people who were thousands of miles away. He would make remarkable diagnoses which were later verified by medical authorities. All this was accomplished in spite of the fact that Cayce had no medical training and only a grammar school education.

Sometimes during his trances he would speak about religious and philosophical issues, and occasionally he would predict the future. During his career his "readings" on medical questions totalled almost 15,000.

Cayce was active in the "Christian" church, faithfully reading his Bible from beginning to end each year for 46 years. However, at the same time, he was an occult practitioner who gained international fame for his exploits.

In 1931 Cayce formed a foundation which he named the Association of Research and Enlightenment, Inc. The purpose of the A.R.E. was the preservation and study of the readings of Edgar Cayce. Cayce's son, Hugh Lynn, assumed leadership of the organization upon his father's death in 1945. The A.R.E. did not stagnate after its founder's death, but instead used his readings and experiences as a vast resource for reaching the contemporary world.

Today's aggressively evangelistic A.R.E. claims to "offer a contemporary and mature view of the reality of extrasensory perception, the importance of dreams, the logic of reincarnation, and a rational or loving personal concept of God, the practical use of prayer and meditation and a deeper understanding of the Bible" (William J. Peterson, *Those Curious New Cults*, New Canaan, CN: Keats Publishing, Inc., 1973, 1975, p. 48). Current paid membership in the A.R.E. totals 20,000.

Cayce's Readings

The readings made by Cayce over the years reveal not only cures for medical ailments, but also statements about God and the future. His readings brought out the following:

- California would fall into the Pacific Ocean in the early 1970's.
- Jesus Christ was a reincarnation of Adam, Melchizedek, Joshua and other figures who lived before Him.
- God has in His nature a male and female principle, making Him a Father-Mother God.
- Mary, the mother of Jesus, was virgin-born like her Son.
- God does not know the future.
- Salvation is something man does on his own. It is not a work of God alone.
- Reincarnation occurs in many human beings.
- Jesus was tutored in prophecy on Mt. Carmel while He was a teenager. His teacher was a woman named Judy, a leader of the Essenes.
- Jesus grew up in Capernaum, not Nazareth.
- Luke did not write the Acts of the Apostles as traditionally believed by the Church. The true author was Cayce himself in a previous life as Lucius, Bishop of Laodicea.

Biblical Evaluation

Although the A.R.E. claims to be a study group and not a religion, the readings made by Cayce comment on God and consequently should be evaluated in the light of God's revealed Word, the Bible.

First and foremost, Edgar Cayce is a false prophet according to biblical standards. He predicted many things which did not come to pass.

> When a prophet speaks in the Name of the Lord, if the thing does not come about or come true, that is the thing which the Lord has not spoken. The prophet has spoken it presumptuously; you shall not be afraid of him (Deuteronomy 18:22, NASB).

When Cayce said God does not know the future, he clearly contradicted Scripture. In stark contrast to Cayce, the God of the Bible does know the future, telling mankind of events before they come to pass.

> I declared the former things long ago and they went forth from my mouth, and I proclaimed them. Suddenly I acted, and they came to pass.... Therefore I declared them to you long ago; before they took place I proclaimed them to you, lest you should say, my idol has done them and my graven image and my molten image have commanded them (Isaiah 48:3, 5, NASB).

The God of the Bible revealed through His prophets many things in detail before they came to pass. The predictions were specific and always accurate. Contrast that to Cayce, whose predictions were vague and often inaccurate.

There is no evidence that Jesus studied prophecy on Mt. Carmel or was a member of the Essenes. The teachings of Jesus came not from men but from God the Father: "Jesus therefore said, 'When you lift up the Son of Man, then you will know that I am He, and I do nothing on my own initiative, but I speak these things as the Father taught me'" (John 8:28, NASB).

Cayce and his followers have a low view of the Person and work of Jesus Christ. One Cayce devotee expressed it this way:

> For almost 20 centuries the moral sense of the Western World has been blunted by a theology which teaches the vicarious

atonement of sin through Christ, the Son of God.... All men and women are sons of God.... Christ's giving of his life...is no unique event in history.... To build these two statements, therefore—that Christ was the Son of God and that he died for man's salvation—into a dogma, and then to make salvation depend upon believing that dogma, has been the great psychological crime because it places responsibility for redemption on something external to the self; it makes salvation dependent on belief in the divinity of another person rather than on self-transformation through belief in one's own intrinsic divinity (quoted in Phillip Swihart, *Reincarnation, Edgar Cayce and the Bible*, Downers Grove, IL: Inter-Varsity Press, 1975, pp. 27, 28).

Cayce's claim to be the reincarnated author of the book of Acts rests on his fundamental belief in reincarnation. This is one of the central doctrines and greatest attractions of the A.R.E. If one disproves reincarnation, the validity of the A.R.E. is forever destroyed. We will examine the claims of reincarnation and compare them to the truths of the Bible.

Reincarnation

One of the oldest of all religious beliefs is that of reincarnation. If one will closely study ancient religions, the teaching of reincarnation will appear frequently in a variety of different forms. The belief in reincarnation, however, is not limited to ancient religions but is widely held today by many different religions, cultic and occultic groups, including the A.R.E.

The idea behind reincarnation is that a person's soul lives a succession of lives which will eventually terminate when that person has, by his deeds, rid himself of all sin. This experience where reincarnation is no longer necessary is known as nirvana in Eastern thought, or becoming one with the divine universe. The person is born, lives and dies and comes back with a new body (hence, reincarnation). This cycle usually continues until that person reaches eternal bliss.

It needs to be mentioned that reincarnation, more a Western concept while still often held in the East, is not the same as the Eastern teaching of transmigration of the soul. The teaching of transmigration of the soul permits the person to return not only in human bodies but also in plants and animals.

While reincarnation is limited to the human body, "transmigration is still the teaching of pure Hinduism, but many offshoots of Hinduism and most Western proponents of such ideas have rejected transmigration and now embrace only reincarnation" (Walter Martin, *The New Cults*, op. cit., p. 352).

Many people turn to the Bible in an attempt to support the idea of reincarnation, but a study of the Scripture will reveal that the Bible is diametrically opposed to reincarnation. Rather than teach that we can have many deaths and rebirths, the Bible makes it clear that there is only one death per person.

But what about the various cases of alleged reincarnation which have been publicized in recent years, some sounding very convincing? One answer to this lies in the spiritual warfare spoken of in Scripture. The Bible says that "we wrestle not with flesh and blood but with principalities and powers and spiritual wickedness in high places" (Ephesians 6:12).

There is a spiritual battle going on, and if people can be convinced that there is no judgment after this life but merely a progression into the next, then they will feel no need to receive Jesus Christ as Savior. We believe it is one of the desires of Satan and his hosts to convince people they must atone for their own sins, and belief in reincarnation is one of these devices.

People experience what they believe is a regression into a past when in actuality their experience is in the realm of the occult. It is easy for demonic forces, which have been around from the beginning of the earth, to reveal to someone some past act or experience. You will always note that any so-called reincarnation experience will lead people away from the God of the Bible and the death of Christ on the cross for the forgiveness of sins.

The possibility of fraud also may be involved in so-called reincarnation experiences. The information brought out during the times of regression could be obtained by other means, such as some research about the person who supposedly is speaking. This type of fraud has been perpetrated with regard to spiritists who have "inside information" about the dead ones who allegedly speak during a seance. In reality the medium has done his homework and thus can impress the participant with little-known information about the dead. The same type of thing happens in many supposed cases of reincarnation.

Reincarnation teaches that only through many lifetimes can one rid himself of the debt for all of his sins. However, the Bible teaches that through Jesus Christ we can be rid of the penalty for all our sins at one time (1 John 1:8-10). His purpose for dying on the cross was as a sacrifice for our sins (Acts 3: 18, 19).

Jesus Christ is the only Savior we ever need because "He abides forever, holds His priesthood permanently. Hence, also, He is able to save forever those who draw near to God through Him, since He always lives to make intercession for them" (Hebrews 7:24, 25, NASB). We have the promise of God Himself that our salvation has been guaranteed through faith in the sacrifice of Jesus Christ on the cross (1 Peter 1:2-6).

As Christians we look forward to resurrection, not reincarnation. Since the fall of man (Genesis 3) the entire universe has been abnormal. Man, animals, nature have all been placed under the sentence of death. God said to Adam, "By the sweat of your face you shall eat bread, till you return to the ground, because from it you were taken, for you are dust, and to dust you shall return" (Genesis 3:19, NASB).

Mankind has always looked forward to something better, namely, a resurrection into a new body on a new planet Earth that has been renovated by God. The Scriptures speak of the time when we shall all be changed:

> Behold I tell you a mystery; we shall not all sleep, but we shall all be changed, in a moment, in the twinkling of an eye, at the last trumpet; for the trumpet will sound, and the dead will be raised imperishable and we shall be changed. For this perishable must put on imperishable and this mortal must put on immortality. But when this perishable will have put on the imperishable, and this mortal will have put on immortality, then will come about the saying that is written, "Death is swallowed up in victory. O death, where is your victory? O death, where is your sting? The sting of death is sin, and the power of sin is the law; but thanks be to God,

who gives us the victory through our Lord Jesus Christ"
(1 Corinthians 15:51-57, NASB).

Elsewhere the Scripture says we shall be made like Him
at the resurrection, "Beloved, now are we children of God,
and it has not appeared as yet what we shall be. We know
that, when He appears, we shall be like Him, because we
shall see Him just as He is" (1 John 3:2, NASB).
Furthermore the whole creation will be made new:

And He shall wipe away every tear from their eyes; and there
shall no longer be any death; there shall no longer be any
mourning, or crying, or pain; the first things have passed
away. And He who sits on the Throne said, "Behold, I am
making all things new" (Revelation 21:4, 5, NASB).

Thus, the Bible gives the believer the promise of a new
body and a new world at the resurrection of the dead. This
can be received by belief in Christ, not through a series of
rebirths as taught by reincarnation.
Clifford Wilson and John Weldon show some of the
differences between Christianity and reincarnation:

Christianity	Reincarnation
Believes in judgment that is eternal, following man's death.	States we have many lives, even thousands, to perfect ourselves.
God judges us.	We only judge ourselves.
Believes in the atonement of Jesus Christ for our sins.	States we need no savior, therefore denies the necessity of salvation; there is no need for it, according to the nature of "reality."
Believes in the existence of hell as a place, eternal.	States everyone will be "saved" (absorbed into the divine) in the end.
Believes in the deity of Christ.	Vague and contradictory views on "God." States there is no need for Jesus to be God—He was just more advanced ("He's been through more incarnations") than most.

Believes in the existence of personal devil or Satan, and fallen evil spirits — demons.	All evil is a result of man's choosing. Satan is devised by human institution. Evil spirits are held to be regressed human spirits between incarnations, not demons.
Believes in the *Bible* as God's *only* Word to mankind.	Opposes biblical concepts: e.g., Hebrews 9:27. *All* religious Scriptures or writings are communications from God or the spirit world to help man.
Believes in a personal God, revealed as the Trinity of Father, Son, and Holy Spirit	Denies a personal triune God. Ultimate reality is often impersonal karmic law.
Believes in Heaven as a distinct, eternal place.	Various progressive spirit-realms.
Believes in the sinlessness of Christ.	Denies it; no one is perfect (some may say Christ has *now* reached perfection, but that He was a sinner like everyone else, beforehand).
Believes in the physical eternal resurrection of Jesus Christ.	Denies it; He will come back in another reincarnation, or He has now no need to come back at all.
Believes in personal resurrection and immortality.	The individual person is forever gone upon the next reincarnation.

(Clifford Wilson and John Weldon, *Occult Shock and Psychic Forces*, San Diego: Master Books, 1980, pp. 86, 87).

Edgar Cayce cannot be considered a prophet of God. Although he faithfully read his Bible and was active in church, his "readings" contradicted every sacred belief of Christianity. The A.R.E. which Cayce founded has continued in his anti-Christian beliefs and should also be avoided.

William Petersen gives a thought-provoking conclusion concerning Cayce's activities:

For a good portion of his life, Cayce was a commercial photographer. He understood very well the mechanics of his trade. A blank film is developed in the dark.

The nature of a photograph, whether it is a formal family picture or pornography, depends not on the film but on the photographer who uses the camera. During his trances, Cayce's mind was like a blank film that would be developed in the dark.

I believe that Cayce allowed his camera to get into the wrong hands (William J. Petersen, op. cit., p. 59).

CHAPTER SIX

Demons

The Bible not only teaches the existence of the devil but also of a great company of his followers known as demons or evil spirits. These demons originally were holy but with the leader, Satan, they fell away from God. Their ultimate end will be eternal damnation when God judges Satan and his host at the Great White Throne judgment (Revelation 20:10-15).

These demons have certain characteristics revealed by the Scripture, including the following:

(1) Demons are spirits without bodies.
For our struggle is not against flesh and blood, but against the rulers, against the powers, against the world forces of this darkness, against the spiritual forces of wickedness in the heavenly places (Ephesians 6:12, NASB).

(2) Demons were originally in fellowship with God.
And angels who did not keep their own domain, but abandoned their proper abode, He has kept in eternal bonds under darkness for the judgment of the great day (Jude 6, NASB).

(3) Demons are numerous.
For He said unto him, "Come out of the man, you unclean spirit!" And He was asking him, "What is your name?" And he said to Him, "My name is Legion; for we are many" (Mark 5:8, 9, NASB).

(4) Demons are organized.
...This man casts out demons only by Beelzebub the ruler of the demons (Matthew 12:24, NASB).

(5) Demons have supernatural powers.

For they are spirits of demons, performing signs, which go out to the kings of the whole world, to gather them together for the war of the Great Day of God, the Almighty (Revelation 16:14, NASB).

(6) Demons are knowledgeable of God.

And behold, they cried out, saying, "What do we have to do with you, Son of God? Have you come here to torment us before the time?" (Mattehw 8:29, NASB).

(7) Demons are allowed to roam the earth and torment unbelievers.

Now when the unclean spirit goes out of a man, it passes through waterless places, seeking rest, and does not find it. Then it says, "I will return to my house from which I came"; and when it comes, it finds it unoccupied, swept and put in order. Then it goes, and takes along with it seven other spirits more wicked than itself, and they go in and live there; and the last state of that man becomes worse than the first (Matthew 12:43-45, NASB).

(8) Demons sometimes can inflict sickness.

And as they were going out, behold a dumb man, demon possessed, was brought to Him. And after the demon was cast out, the dumb man spoke... (Matthew 9:32, 33, NASB).

(9) Demons can possess or control animals.

And He gave them permission. And coming out, the unclean spirits entered the swine; and the herd rushed down the steep bank into the sea, about two thousand of them, and they were drowned in the sea (Mark 5:13, NASB).

(10) Demons can possess or control human beings.

And also some women who had been healed of evil spirits and sicknesses; Mary who was called Magdalene, from whom seven demons had gone out (Luke 8:2, NASB).

(11) Demons sometimes can cause mental disorders.

And when He had come out of the boat, immediately a man from the tombs with an unclean spirit met Him and he had his dwelling among the tombs. And no one was able to bind him anymore, even with a chain... and constantly night and day among the tombs and in the mountains, he was crying out and gashing himself with stones (Mark 5:2, 3, 5, NASB).

(12) Demons know that Jesus Christ is God.

And just then there was in their synagogue a man with an unclean spirit; and he cried out, saying, "What do we

have to do with you, Jesus of Nazareth? Have you come
to destroy us? I know who you are—the Holy One of
God" (Mark 1:23, 24, NASB).

(13) Demons tremble before God.
You believe that God is one. You do well; the demons
also believe, and shudder (James 2:19, NASB).

(14) Demons teach false doctrine.
But the Spirit explicitly says that in later times some will
fall away from the faith, paying attention to deceitful
spirits and doctrines of demons (1 Timothy 4:1, NASB).

(15) Demons oppose God's people.
For our struggle is not against flesh and blood, but against
the rulers, against the powers, against the world forces of
this darkness, against the spiritual forces of wickedness
in the heavenly places (Ephesians 6:12, NASB).

(16) Demons attempt to destroy Christ's Kingdom.
Be of sober spirit, be on the alert. Your adversary, the
devil, prowls about like a roaring lion, seeking someone
to devour (1 Peter 5:8, NASB).

(17) God takes advantage of the actions of demons to accomplish His divine purposes.
Then God sent an evil spirit between Abimelech and the
men of Shechem; and the men of Shechem dealt
treacherously with Abimelech (Judges 9:23, NASB).

(18) God is going to judge demons at the last judgment.
For if God did not spare angels when they sinned, but
cast them into hell and committed them to pits of
darkness, reserved for judgment... (2 Peter 2:4, NASB).

Demon Possession

Since the release of the motion picture, "The Exorcist,"
there has been renewed discussion about the subject of
demon possession. Can demon possession, or control of a
person's will by a demon, actually occur? What are the
signs of a possessed person? Is it really just superstition
and ignorance to believe in demon possession? Because of
the continual interest in these and other questions, we felt
we should address the subject of demon possession.

The Reality of Demon Possession

The evidence from Scripture is *unmistakable* that a
human being can be possessed or controlled by a demon or
evil spirit (Mark 7:24-30, 9:17-29).

From the New Testament accounts of demon possession, along with other examples, we can chart some of the phenomena that can be observed during a demonic attack.

A. Change of Personality
Including intelligence, moral character, demeanor, appearance.

B. Physical Changes
1. Preternatural strength
2. Epileptic convulsions; foaming
3. Catatonic symptoms, falling
4. Clouding of consciousness, anaesthesia to pain
5. Changed voice

C. Mental Changes
1. Glossolalia; understanding unknown languages [the counterfeit gift as opposed to the biblical gift].
2. Preternatural knowledge
3. Psychic and occult powers, e.g., clairvoyance, telepathy and prediction

D. Spiritual Changes
1. Reaction to and fear of Christ; blasphemy with regret as in depression
2. Affected by prayer

E. Deliverance possible in the name of Jesus
As this is a diagnosis in retrospect it falls outside the range of pre-exorcism symptoms. (John Richards, *But Deliver Us From Evil: An Introduction to the Demonic Dimension in Pastoral Care*, London: Darton, Longman and Todd, 1974, p. 156).

Does Demon Possession Occur Today?

Granting the fact that demon possession occurred in New Testament times, the natural question arises, "Does it occur today?" After extensive study of demonology and years of observing patients, psychiatrist Paul Meier gives his professional opinion:

I can honestly say that I have never yet seen a single case of demon possession. The main thing I have learned about demon possession is how little we really know about it and how little the Bible says about it.

I have had hundreds of patients who came to see me because they thought they were demon possessed. Scores of them heard "demon voices" telling them evil things to do. It was at first surprising to me that all of these had dopamine deficiencies in their brains, which were readily correctable with Thorazine or any other major tranquilizer. I discovered that all of the "demons" I was seeing were allergic to Thorazine and that, in nearly every case, a week or two on Thorazine made the "demons" go away and brought the patient closer to his real conflicts. These demons were merely auditory hallucinations. To have self-esteem, these patients were unconsciously amplifying their own unwanted thoughts so loud they seemed like real voices. They felt less guilty when they could convince themselves that these thoughts were coming from an external source ("demons"), rather than from within themselves.

Don't get me wrong, I am a strict Biblicist who believes in the inerrancy of Scripture. I believe demons really do exist because the Bible says they do. I believe that there probably are some demon possessed persons in various parts of the world (Danny Korem and Paul Meier, *The Fakers*, Grand Rapids, MI: Baker Book House, 1980, pp. 160, 161).

However, there are many others who attest to having witnessed demon possession. Kurt Koch* writes, "I was once invited by Dr. Martin Lloyd-Jones to speak before a group of psychiatrists in London. During the discussion which followed my talk, two psychiatrists stood up and stated quite dogmatically that possession as such did not exist. Immediately after this, however, two other psychiatrists present—they were both Christians—rose to their feet and said that they were not only convinced that possession was a genuine phenomenon, but that they had already come across cases of it within their own practice, one of them seven cases and the other eleven" (Kurt Koch, *Demonology, Past and Present*, Grand Rapids, MI: Kregel Publications, 1973, p. 32.)

In the 19th century there were some striking cases of demon possession recorded in China by missionary John L. Nevius. When Nevius first came to China, he firmly

---

* In this volume we will refer quite often to the examples of occultic activity documented in the writings of Kurt Koch. The authors do this because Koch is the most well-known writer on the subject of the occult in the evangelical Christian world. However, citing his examples does not necessarily mean that we come to the same conclusions or agree that his examples are clear indications of occultic activity.

believed that demons belonged to a bygone era. When he heard firsthand accounts of demon possession, he considered it superstition. However, try as he would, he could not convince the people that what they had heard and seen was a result of their imaginations. Finally, the evidence led him to a change of mind, not only believing the demons existed but also that demon possession was in fact a present reality.

Nevius said this of his experiences:

> I brought with me to China a strong conviction that a belief in demons, and communications with spiritual beings, belongs exclusively to a barbarous and superstitious age, and at present can consist only with mental weakness and want of culture. I indulged Mr. Tu (his Chinese teacher), however, in talking on his favorite topics, because he did so with peculiar fluency and zest, and thus, elements of variety and novelty were utililzed in our severe and otherwise monotonous studies. But Mr. Tu's marvelous stories soon lost the charm of novelty. I used my best endeavors, though with little success, to convince him that his views were not the combined result of ignorance and imagination. I could not but notice, however, the striking resemblance between some of his statements of alleged facts and the demonology of Scripture. This resemblance I account for only as apparent or accidental.... (John L. Nevius, *Demon Possession*, Grand Rapids, MI: Kregel Publications, 1968, pp. 9, 10).

Nevius then records his many and varied experiences with demon possessed people which eventually led to his change of mind on the matter.

Walter Martin gives a couple of examples of demon possession he has encountered:

> Recently in the San Fernando Valley of California three husky clergymen tried to hold down a 120-pound girl who was possessed with multiple demons. She successfully resisted all three of them for a number of minutes, until she was finally subdued. However, she was still able to kick one man's shins until they were bloody, demonstrating tremendous supernatural power.
>
> In Newport Beach, California, I encountered a case of demonic possession in which five persons, including myself, were involved. In this case the girl, who was about 5 feet 4 inches tall and weighed 120 pounds, attacked a 180-pound man and with one arm flipped him 5 or 6 feet away. It took

four of us, including her husband, to hold her body to a bed while we prayed in the name of Jesus Christ for the exorcism of the demons within her.

During the course of the exorcism we found out that she was possessed because she had worshipped Satan, and because of that worship he had come with his forces and taken control of her. She was a perfect "tare in the wheat field," as Jesus said (Matthew 13:24-30). She had married a Christian, was a daughter of a Christian minister, had taught Sunday school in a Christian church, and had appeared on the surface to be perfectly consistent with Christian theology. But the whole time she was laughing inwardly at the church and at Christ. It was not until her exorcism that she was delivered and received Jesus Christ as her Lord and Savior. Today she and her husband are on the mission field serving the Lord Jesus Christ.

I have a psychologist friend who was present with me at an exorcism in Newport Beach, California. Before we entered the room he said, "I want you to know I do not believe in demonic possession. This girl is mentally disturbed."

I said, "That may well be. We'll find out very soon."

As we went into the room and closed the door, the girl's supernatural strength was soon revealed. Suddenly from her body a totally foreign voice said quietly, with a smirk on the face (she was unconscious—the psychologist testified to that), "We will outlast you."

The psychologist looked at me and said, "What was that?"

"That is what you don't believe in," I said.

We spent about 3½ hours exorcising what the psychologist didn't believe in!

At the end of the exorcism he was not only a devout believer in the personality of the devil, but in demonic possession and biblical exorcism as well. He now knows that there are other-dimensional beings capable of penetrating this dimension and of controlling human beings! (Walter Martin, *Exorcism: Fact or Fable*, Santa Ana, CA: Vision House Publishers, 1975, pp. 17, 18, 21).

In conclusion, although most cases of alleged demon possession turn out to be in reality something quite different, it does not negate the fact that demon possession can and does occur today. However, one should be very careful before he considers an individual demon possessed when the person's problem may be physiological or psychological.

Only a mature Christian, experienced and seasoned by

the Lord in counseling and spiritual warfare, should take an active part in diagnosing or treating alleged cases of demon possession. The human body, mind and spirit is so complex and interrelated that it takes spiritual discernment coupled with a great amount of knowledge to deal responsibly with what appears to be demon possession.

If you know of someone who appears to be demon possessed and who wants help, you can and should pray for him and direct him to someone who is qualified to help. There is hope for him: God can and will set him free from whatever is binding him, be it demonic, physiological or psychological.

NOTE: The subject of the believer and demon possession will be dealt with in a later volume.

CHAPTER SEVEN

Jeane Dixon

I nvariably when the subject of astrology is discussed, the question of Jeane Dixon is brought up. Is Jeane Dixon a true prophetess? Do her powers come from God? What about the amazing predictions that she has made? We feel these and other questions concerning Jeane Dixon need to be addressed in light of the Bible in order to get a true picture of the situation.

Background

Jeane Dixon was born Jeane-(or Lydia) Pinckert around the turn of the century in a small Wisconsin town. Her psychic abilities were either non-existent or hidden during her early years. It was not until she met a gypsy woman who gave her a crystal ball that her psychic career began.

Supposedly, this gypsy woman told her she had the makings of a psychic, destined for great things. Although she received recognition as early as the forties for her psychic powers, it was the publication of two books concerning her life, *A Gift of Prophecy* by Ruth Mont-gomery in 1965, and *Jeane Dixon, My Life and Prophecies* by Rene Noorbergen in 1969, that made her famous.

The Claims of Jeane Dixon

Jeane Dixon has made it clear that she believes her prophetic gift comes from God. "It is my belief God has given me a gift of prophecy for His own reasons, and I do not question them" (Jeane Dixon, *The Call to Glory*, New York: William Morrow & Company, 1972, p. 42).

Furthermore, she has stated, "The future has been shown me to 2037 A.D." (ibid, p. 175). She told her biographer, Rene Noorbergen, that, "The same spirit that worked through Isaiah and John the Baptist also works through me" (Rene Noorbergen, *The Soul Hustlers*, Zondervan, 1976, p. 114).

In the foreword of her book, *The Gift of Prophecy*, Ruth Montgomery designated Mrs. Dixon as a "modern-day psychic whose visions apparently lift the curtain of tomorrow."

Fulfilled Prophecies?

Mrs. Dixon and others have made some astounding claims as to her ability to predict the future. The introductory section of one of her books reads as follows:

> If you don't believe that anyone can predict the future with a crystal ball...then read these startling, often frightening, precognitions of events by the phenomenal Jeane Dixon.
>
> — The assassination of President Kennedy...
> — Nehru's death and his succession by Shastri
> — That China would go communistic
> — The assassination of Mahatma Ghandi
> — Russia's launching the world's first satellite
> — Eisenhower's election; his heart attack, and his recovery
> — The Kremlin shake-up ending with Krushchev's dismissal and Suslov's takeover (Ruth Montgomery, *A Gift of Prophecy*, New York: Bantam Books, 1970, Preface).

She also supposedly predicted the deaths of Carole Lombard and Marilyn Monroe and the assassinations of Robert F. Kennedy and Martin Luther King.

In the May 13, 1956 issue of *Parade Magazine*, she made this prophecy:

> As to the 1960 election, Mrs. Dixon thinks it will be dominated by labor and won by a Democrat. But he will be assassinated or die in office, though not necessarily in his first term.

With these examples of fulfilled prophecy, one might conclude that Jeane Dixon has a true prophetic gift.

However, upon closer examination her "amazing" prophecies are not really that amazing. On her prophecy concerning the 1960 Presidential election, Milbourne Cristopher comments:

> As we know now, the election was not "dominated by labor." She did not name the Democrat she said would win; no date was given for the president-to-be's end; and his announced demise was qualified with Delphic ingenuity "assassinated or die in office, though not necessarily in his first term." Thus if the president served a single term, it would be within four years; if he was re-elected there was an eight-year span.
>
> Such a surmise was not illogical for anyone who has studied recent American history. William McKinley was assassinated a year after the turn of the century. Warren Gamaliel Harding and Franklin Delano Roosevelt died in office, and during Harry S. Truman's tenure an attempt was made on his life. Moreover, the normal burdens of the presidency are such that it is commonly regarded as a man-killing office. Woodrow Wilson and Dwight Eisenhower were critically ill during their terms. Unfortunately for the nation, the odds against Mrs. Dixon's prophecy's being fulfilled were not too great — 7-3 based on 20th century experience (Milbourne Cristopher, *ESP, Seers and Psychics*, New York: Thomas Crowell Co., 1970, pp. 80, 81).

Moreover, before the 1960 election, Mrs. Dixon changed her mind, as Cristopher points out:

> In January 1960 Mrs. Dixon changed her mind. Kennedy, then a contender for the Democrat nomination, would not be elected in November, she said in Ruth Montgomery's syndicated column. In June she stated that "the symbol of the Presidency is directly over the head of Vice-President Nixon" but "unless the Republican party really gets out and puts forth every effort it will topple." Fire enough shots, riflemen agree, and eventually you will hit the bull's-eye (ibid, p. 81).

One of the most famous of all her prophecies was received on February 5, 1962. "A child, born somewhere in the Middle East shortly after 7 a.m. (EST) on February 5, 1962 will revolutionize the world. Before the close of the century he will bring together all mankind in one all-embracing faith. This will be the foundation of a new Christianity, with every sect and creed united through this man who will walk among the people to spread the wisdom of the Almighty Power...He is the answer to the prayers of a troubled world."

This prophecy of a coming Messiah who would save the world received much criticism. Consequently, Mrs. Dixon revised the true identity of this child. Her biographer, Rene Noorbergen, notes:

> For several years Jeane continued to advocate that this Christ-child would guide the world in the early 1980s. The child was godly, he was divine, and he would become the salvation of the world.
>   Suddenly something happened.
>   While interviewing "Mrs. D" for *My Life and Prophecies*, I became aware of the inconsistencies in the revelation. Over-sensitive to criticism, Mrs. Dixon soon changed her interpretation. "There is no doubt that he will fuse multitudes into one all-embracing doctrine," she explained in her "revised version." She continued, "He will form a new 'Christianity' based on his 'almighty power,' but leading man in a direction far removed from the teachings and life of Christ, the Son." Enlarging on her new interpretation, she called the child the "Antichrist"—a far cry from her first prophetic evaluation (Rene Noorbergen, *The Soul Hustlers*, Zondervan, 1976, p. 121).

False Prophecies

Although Jeane Dixon supposedly has made some predictions that have come true, she has made many other prophecies that have failed. These include:

(1) World War III would begin in 1954;

(2) Red China would be admitted to the United Nations in 1958, yet this did not occur until 1971;

(3) The Vietnam war would end in 1966, yet it did not end until 1975;

(4) On October 19, 1968, she predicted Jacqueline Kennedy was not thinking of marriage and the next day Mrs. Kennedy married Aristotle Onassis!

(5) Union Leader, Walter Reuther, would run for President in 1964, which he did not do.

(6) In 1970, she predicted the following events which did not occur:

  (a) Castro would be overthrown from Cuba and would have to leave the island;

  (b) New facts concerning the death of President Ken-

nedy would be brought to light from a foreign source;
  (c) Attempts would be made on the life of President
      Nixon;
(7) In 1971, she made the following predictions, neither one
    of which has come true:
    (a) Both Anwar Sadat of Egypt and King Hussein of
        Jordan would lose their thrones;
    (b) Russia would be the first nation to put men on the
        moon;
(8) She has made other predictions that have not yet come
    true, including:
    (a) The Berlin Wall will come down;
    (b) Red China will invade Russia;
    (c) Russia will ally with the United States.

Evaluation

There are those who believe Jeane Dixon has no
supernatural power whatsoever but is rather a clever
fortuneteller. Danny Korem comments:

> In a given population there will be those whose "hit" ratio (a
> thought and an event matching up) will be higher than others
> simply because of the law of probability. This is true in any
> game of chance. When a clever fortuneteller combines good
> cold-reading techniques with a chance guess or two, he or she
> will appear to almost unerringly pick up someone's thoughts
> and prognosticate the future, but there will be other times
> when he or she will fail. My question is this: If such powers
> exist, why are they so fleeting, and why can't they be tested?
> The reason is a simple one. They don't exist. In the 12 years I
> have devoted to researching this subject, I have neither seen a
> valid case of prognostication, nor have I been confronted with
> hard-core documentation to substantiate a purported case
> (Danny Korem and Paul Meier, *The Fakers*, Grand Rapids,
> MI: Baker Book House, 1980, p. 115).

Whether Mrs. Dixon possesses a supernatural ability to
predict the future or not, she is definitely not a prophet of
God for she fails on the following counts:
  (1) *The Use of Occult Artifacts.*
Jeane Dixon uses such things as a crystal ball, a deck of
tarot cards and other occult artifacts to receive her
prophecies. This type of practice is at odds with Scripture,
for the biblical prophets received their prophecies directly
from God without the use of any artifacts. The artifacts

Mrs. Dixon uses are the same ones used by fortune tellers who attempt to predict the future through occultic means. A true prophet of God would never resort to using any occultic paraphernalia.

The true prophet of God spoke by the direct agency of God through the power of the Holy Spirit, not by means of any occultic devices. The words of the prophets are preserved for us in Holy Scripture (Romans 1:2) and their supreme testimony is always of Jesus Christ, the Son of God (Hebrews 1:1, 2).

(2) *Her Prophecies Do Not Exalt Jesus Christ.*

The Bible makes it clear that all true prophecy has Jesus Christ as its central theme, "...for the testimony of Jesus is the Spirit of prophecy" (Revelation 19:10, NASB).

Mrs. Dixon fails miserably in this, for there is no attempt in her prophecies to bring people to the God of the Bible and His Son, Jesus Christ. There is simply no witness to Christ in her prophecies! Moreover, many of her prophecies concern such commonplace things as what television show will be popular or the latest fashions. These are given without any spiritual meaning whatsoever and do not direct one's attention to the Gospel of Christ.

The biblical prophets always prophesied in accordance with God's will and for His glory. There is no room for frivolous and gossiping prophecy in God's Word.

Mrs. Dixon does no such thing. The biblical prophets also gave their prophecies in the Name of the Lord, something Jeane Dixon does not do. Since Jeane Dixon does not prophesy in the Name of the Lord or for the purpose of bringing individuals into a personal relationship with Christ, she cannot be considered a true prophet of God.

(3) *She Gives Prophecies That Do Not Come True.*

Mrs. Dixon also fails in the most important test of all: She utters prophecies which do not come true. The Bible makes it clear how one can know who is a true prophet of God: "And you may say in your heart, 'How shall we know the word which the Lord has not spoken?' When a prophet speaks in the Name of the Lord, if the thing does not come about or come true, that is the thing which the Lord has not spoken. The prophet has spoken it presumptuously;

you shall not be afraid of him" (Deuteronomy 18:21, 22, NASB).

Mrs. Dixon, as we have already documented, has made a great many predictions that did not come to pass. To qualify for being a false prophet, a person need make only one false prophecy, for a true prophet of God will not make any mistakes in predicting the future. Jeane Dixon uses occultic artifacts in her predicting. She does not speak in the Name of the Lord, neither does she exalt Jesus Christ in her prophetic utterances. She has predicted many things that have failed to materialize. Consequently, she cannot be considered a prophet of the true and living God.

CHAPTER EIGHT

Dowsing

Dowsing is the search for and location of underground springs and other objects beneath the ground by the use of a divining rod. The divining rod is a V-shaped wooden twig or piece of wire from six to eighteen inches in length which is used by the dowser, the person who possesses this ability to search for underground objects. The rod is held firmly in the hands of the dowser until the force coming from the underground object causes the rod to snap over.

Does dowsing work? Milbourne Cristopher states,

> P. A. Ongley reported in the New Zealand Journal of Science and Technology, in 1948, that fifty-eight dowsers participated in tests devised to determine their ability to make the same spots they had indicated with their eyes open when their eyes were closed, to tell if buried bottles containing water, and otherwise give evidence of their purported powers. Their scores were on pure-chance levels. Seventeen other diviners who specialize in diverse fields were observed. As in the earlier experiments in France, seven illness detectors found twenty-five diseases in a patient who doctors said was healthy, and one diviner, whose eyes were bandaged, said the leg over which he worked had varicose veins. Actually it was an artificial limb (Milbourne Cristopher, *ESP, Seers and Psychics*, New York: Thomas Y. Crowell Co., p. 140).

In his discussion of divining rods, Herbert Leventhal states:

A second major feature of these tales is their association of dowsing with a host of other occult and supernatural phenomena. By combining the various accounts, a common pattern of American treasure-hunting magic can be discovered. The treasure is located by a divining rod, which sometimes contained mercury or was prepared at an especially propitious time; one or more protective circles, a common feature of European ceremonial magic, are drawn; magical charms, or religious verses used as charms, are recited to overcome the guardian spirits; and nails or metal rods are sometimes used to pin down the treasure because... treasure was wont to move about and attempt to escape.

Some of the other stories, especially those recorded only in nineteenth-century secondary sources, may well have been influenced by the generally accepted theme for magical treasure hunting, but the existence of this theme itself indicates a general knowledge of dowsing, and enough evidence remains to leave no doubt that dowsing for treasure, including appropriate protective measures against hostile spirits, was a not unusual occurrence in eighteenth-century America (Herbert Leventhal, *In the Shadow of the Enlightenment: Occultism and Renaissance Science in Eighteenth-Century America*, New York: New York University Press, 1976, pp. 117, 118).

Some practitioners of dowsing seem actually to have the ability to find water. How is this to be explained? Some believe that Satan empowers the dowser supernaturally to find the water or object desired. While this is possible, there seems to be a better explanation.

There are those individuals, however, who do display an uncanny ability to discover water by means of dowsing. Mr. Rawcliffe, in his book *Occult and Supernatural Phenomena* points out, after exhaustive research, that there are subtle surface clues that may allow one to discern where underground streams or pockets of water may exist. The following is only a partial list of surface clues that may subconsciously aid the dowser: (1) naturally absorbent substratum and subsoil; (2) growth of vegetation; (3) temperature of surrounding air; (4) smell of damp earth; (5) underground streams audible to the ear; and (6) ground vibrations due to underground stream. It must be noted that most clues are very subtle and, for the most part, are registered subliminally by the dowser and then translated by ideomotor action into the dipping of the rod. (Danny Korem and Paul Meier, *The Fakers*, Grand Rapids, MI: Baker Book House, 1980, p. 57).

Dowsing has never established itself as being scientifically credible because all controlled experiments do not point to any remarkable accuracy of the dowsers. Those who do seem to have an ability to find water underground are most likely responding subconsciously to the surface clues.

In addition, we should note that many people who become involved in dowsing (sometimes called water-witching) also become involved in other activities that are more directly occultic. It seems to be a step on the way to serious occultic involvement. Since it has no basis scientifically or biblically, and can be a step to occultism, Christians should definitely stay away from it.

CHAPTER NINE

Fire Walking

Fire walking is an ancient practice of someone walking barefoot across a fiery bed of coals or stones without the slightest pain or any damage to the person. It is still widely practiced today in Japan, India and the Fiji Islands.

Since some magicians can duplicate fire walking by trickery, some people dismiss all fire walking as trickery. The trick is accomplished by relying upon short contact with the hot stones which prevents the walker from being burned.

Danny Korem comments, "It has been found that one cannot take more than four steps across a bed of coals without running the risk of being burned. In 1937, Ahmed Hussain, another coal walker, took six steps in 2.3 seconds to cross a 20-foot pit (temperature 740 degrees Celsius) and was severely burned. There have been other laymen, however, who have successfully duplicated the coal-walking stunt.

"Walking on heated stones is even easier, since stone is a poor conductor of heat. You will not, however, witness a fakir walk across a heated steel plate, as steel is an excellent conductor of heat" (Danny Korem and Paul Meier, *The Fakers*, Grand Rapids, MI: Baker Book House, 1980, p. 89).

There are others who see fire walking not as a magician's trick but rather as an occultic practice. This is the position of Kurt Koch, who writes:

In Japan a former fire walker came to me to be counseled. He confessed to his former activities and said that he had really deceived the audience. The fire had been made on a high platform down the center of which there had been a narrow path. Either side of this path was a fire of wood coals. The people around and below the platform had not been able to see the path through the fire. I asked this man if he thought all fire walking was faked in the same way. He replied, "No. Most of it is genuine. It is only faked sometimes for the sake of the tourists."

In South Africa another fire walker confessed to his occult practice. The man was an Indian who worked on a sugar plantation. He told me that he could really walk through fire. He would prepare himself for some days through fasting and meditation, abstaining from alcohol and sexual intercourse, eating only a vegetarian diet, etc. I asked him if he thought the powers he possessed over fire originated from his own subconscious mind. "That's impossible," he replied. "The devil gives this power to those who serve him." He went on to confess that when he had become a Christian he had lost his power to walk through fire.

I know that hypnosis and trance states can protect fire walkers from the pain, but they cannot protect a person from being burnt. One day in India a young mother walked through fire with her small baby. However, she was not fully prepared for the ordeal. Her baby fell from her arms into the fire and was dead within a few seconds. Before the people could reach it, its body was burnt to ashes.

Behind the phenomenon of genuine fire walking there are demonic forces at work, and newly born Christians can feel this in the atmosphere (Kurt Koch, *The Devil's Alphabet*, Grand Rapids, MI: Kregel Publications, pp. 54, 55).

Is there fire walking in the Bible? The Bible gives an account (Daniel 3:21-29) of three men of God who were supernaturally protected when they were thrown into a burning furnace. The Lord God of the Bible protected them because they were being punished for refusing to worship false gods. There are some who try to say this is an example for and justification of fire walking. By reading the account in Daniel, you can see that there is no parallel. The three men of God were preserved to bring glory and honor to the true God, not to amuse onlookers and make the performers rich. One who points to Daniel 3 as justification of fire walking makes a mockery of God's Word.

In conclusion it seems difficult to place all cases of fire walking in the category of trickery or self-hypnosis. But whatever the case may be, fire walking is an ungodly ritual attempting to get the eyes of the observers away from the true and living god. Some see this practice as Satan's imitation of God's miracle in delivering the three Jews from the fiery furnace, showing that the devil has equal power. This, as we have seen, is not the case.

CHAPTER TEN

Fortunetelling

Fortunetelling, the art of forecasting the future supposedly by supernatural means, is an ancient practice which is still popular today. Fortunetelling is also known as divination. The one who practices this activity is known as a diviner. The diviner makes use of various props to receive his supernatural knowledge, including palmistry, cartomancy, mirror mantic and psychometry.

Kurt Koch testifies to the negative result that fortunetelling has on peoples' lives because he sees it as being completely occultic.

...People infected or burdened by fortunetelling and occult phenomena very frequently suffer in the following ways:

The characters of such people reveal abnormal passions, instability, violent tempers, addiction to alcohol, nicotine and sexual vices, selfishness, gossiping, egotism, cursing, etc.

Their religious lives reveal on the one hand an antagonism toward religion, callousness, skepticism, a vicious critical attitude and an inability to pray or read the Bible if they are an atheistic type of person, while on the other hand the pious type reveals a self-righteousness, a spiritual pride, phariseeism, hypocrisy and an insensitivity to the workings of the Holy Spirit.

Medically speaking the families of those involved in fortunetelling reveal in a remarkable way such things as nervous disturbances, psychopathic and hysteric symptoms, cases of St. Vitus' dance, symptoms of paralysis, epileptics, freaks, deaf-mutes, cases of mediumistic psychoses, and a general tendency toward emotional and mental illnesses, etc. (Kurt Koch, *Between Christ and Satan*, Grand Rapids, MI: Kregel Publications, 1968, pp. 49, 50).

There are those who see fortunetelling as a con game without any supernatural phenomena occurring. The fortuneteller, rather than making contact with the spirit world, is a con artist duping the unsuspecting victims. Danny Korem lists certain techniques used by fortunetellers which give realism to their readings:

(1) Observation of sensory clues.

(2) Prior knowledge of subject obtained secretly before reading.

(3) Ability to think on one's feet and change direction of the reading without hesitation or detection.

(4) Understanding of human nature.

(5) Utilization of the cards or any other apparatus to pick up sensory clues or change the direction of the reading when off the track.

(6) An element of luck and a keen sense of playing the odds so that a well-placed guess may produce spectacular results (Danny Korem and Paul Meier, *The Fakers*, Grand Rapids, MI: Baker Book House, 1980, p. 107).

Whether all fortunetelling practice is nothing but a glorified con game remains a matter of debate. What is not debatable is the fact that any and all types of attempting to divine the future through fortunetelling is an abomination to God. God has already revealed to us in His Word the basic program for the future, and He condemns in the strongest of terms those who would try to find out what is going to occur without consulting Him.

The Bible *never* says fortunetellers can predict the future. It is their attempt to peer into the future through occultic means that is objectionable. However, whether they can do it or not really does not make that much difference, if the person having his fortune told believes that they can. The same end is accomplished. The person, instead of looking to God for direction, now consults fortunetellers to receive guidance for his life.

Satan has accomplished his purpose, which is getting people away from worshiping the true and living God.

Since fortunetelling does this, it should never be practiced even for fun. It is a device of the devil which takes one further away from the Kingdom of God. 1 Chronicles 10:13, 14 (NASB) records God's punishment on Saul for going to a medium instead of God:

> So Saul died for his trespass which he committed against the Lord, because of the word of the Lord which he did not keep; and also because he asked counsel of a medium, making inquiry of it, and did not inquire of the Lord. Therefore He killed him, and turned the kingdom to David the son of Jesse.

Some would put fortunetelling in the area of the divine, insisting God had given the fortunetellers their ability. However, this could not be the case since Scripture condemns such practices.

Palmistry (Chiromancy)

Palmistry, or chiromancy, is the art of divination from the shape and markings of the hands and fingers. A proper interpretation of these signs supposedly can be used to forecast the future. It is not to be confused with chirology, which is the scientific study of the development of the shape and lines of the hand, or with graphology, which is handwriting analysis.

Kurt Koch explains chiromancy:

> Here we have fortunetelling by study of the hands. The hand is divided into areas and lines. There is a lunar mountain, the Venus belt, the Martian plain, and areas for spirit, fortune, success, fame, imagination, will and sensuousness. Further, there are four lines which dominate the surface of the palm: the head line, the heart line, the profession line and the life line. From these indications palmists claim to divine and foretell the future (Kurt Koch, *Christian Counseling and Occultism*, Grand Rapids, MI: Kregel Publications, 1972, p. 85).

Unfortunately, palmistry suffers from the same types of verification problems as does astrology. There is no testable, scientific evidence that it works. Lack of documentation and testability have led the scientific community to brand it as mere superstition. The so-called examples of palmistry being able to predict the future have never been substantiated as being right any more often than pure chance would already allow.

As far as trying to justify palmistry from the Bible is concerned, the cause is a hopeless one. The out-of-context verses used by some have nothing to do with palm reading. Moreover, the Scriptures speak loudly and clearly against trying to foretell the future using any form of divination. The following Scripture would apply to palmistry:

> There shall not be found among you anyone who makes his son or daughter pass through the fire, one who uses divination, one who practices witchcraft, or one who interprets omens, or a sorcerer, or one who casts a spell, or a medium, or a spiritist, or one who calls up the dead. For whoever does these things is detestable to the Lord; and because of these detestable things the Lord your God will drive them out before you (Deuteronomy 18:10-12, NASB).

Cartomancy (Tarot Cards)

Cartomancy forecasts the future by means of using cards. The elaborately illustrated cards used in this technique are called Tarot cards. Supposedly these cards hold the secrets to the future.

Those who use the cards extol their virtues:

> The tarot is one of the most wonderful of human inventions. Despite all the outcries of philosophers, this pack of pictures, in which destiny is reflected as a mirror with multiple facets, remains so vital and exercises so irresistible an attraction on imaginative minds that it is hardly possible that austere critics who speak in the name of an exact but uninteresting logic should ever succeed in abolishing its employment (Grillot de Givry, *Witchcraft, Magic and Alchemy*, New York: Dover Publ., 1971, p. 280).

Wheatly offers this explanation:

> Telling fortunes by cards is at the present day probably the most popuar method of predicting a person's future.
>
> There are two distinct types of pack: the Tarot, or Major Arcana, which consists of twenty-two pictorial cards, none of which has any obvious relation to the others; and the Minor Arcana, which originally had fifty-six cards (in modern times reduced to fifty-two) divided into four suits. The suits, now diamonds, hearts, spades and clubs, were originally coins, cups, swords and staffs, which represented respectively commerce, spirituality, war and agriculture. In the old packs the fourteenth card in each suit was the Knight, who has

since been dropped or, if one prefers, merged with the Knave, who represents the squire of the Lord (King) and Lady (Queen). The origin of both packs is lost in mystery. Some writers have stated that the Tarot is the Book of Thoth, the God of Wisdom of the Egyptians; others connect it with the twenty-two paths of the Hebrew Cabala, and still others assert that cards were introduced into western Europe by the Bohemians (Dennis Wheatley, *The Devil and All His Works*, New York: American Heritage Press, 1971, p. 62).

Those who turn to Tarot readings are often insecure about the future. Not content to trust in the providence of God, they anxiously seek forbidden knowledge about the future in the hopes that such knowledge will enable them to escape some impending doom or fate.

There is nothing scientific about Tarot cards. Although fantastic claims have been made for their powers through the centuries, no one has been able to produce significant evidence that such readings are reliable. While we would agree that the majority of Tarot readings are completely fictitious, and depend more on the medium's ability to guess human nature than on spirit guides, there are some readings that appear to be genuinely supernatural.

Since these readings invariably lead a person away from the God of the Bible, and attempt to invade areas of knowledge God has determined should remain secret, we must conclude that they are demonic.

As Christians we can remain confident and peaceful, knowing that God is in full control of our unseen future. Jesus Christ is the only answer for one who is anxious about his future. He said:

> But if God so arrays the grass of the field, which is alive today and tomorrow is thrown into the furnace, will He not much more do so for you, O men of little faith? Do not be anxious then, saying, "What shall we eat?" or "What shall we drink?" or "With what shall we clothe ourselves?" For all of these things the Gentiles eagerly seek; for your heavenly Father knows that you need all these things. But seek first His kingdom and His righteousness; and all these things shall be added to you. Therefore do not be anxious for tomorrow; for tomorrow will care for itself. Each day has enough trouble of its own (Matthew 6:30-34, NASB).

Mirror Mantic

Mirror mantic uses crystal balls, mirrors, rock crystals or still water as "mirrors of the future."

There are in existence occult text books on the subject of mirror mantic and mirror magic. The mirror magician with the help of a magic mirror may attempt to heal or to persecute through magic, to treat people at a distance or to use love and defense magic, and so on. Mirror mantic is often directed at discovering things unknown to the inquirer, in uncovering crimes or diagnosing difficult diseases, and it can embrace any physical event which happens in the world. Mirrors are not the only occult tools used in this field, but crystal balls, rock crystal and other reflecting objects all play a part. Some even use water as a reflecting surface (Kurt Koch, *Between Christ and Satan*, op. cit., p. 42).

This is an ancient method of divination. The one gazing into the crystal supposedly enters a state of clairvoyance where he can see events and things happening at the present or the future, regardless of distance from the diviner. The crystal supposedly enables the person to see a series of pictures of what is taking place or will take place, thus enabling him to peer into the unknown.

Mirror mantic has no foundation in Christianity or science. Rather than being a "window on the future," it is most often just the product of good guessing and a rich imagination on the part of the diviner. In a few cases, genuine occultic involvement appears to take place.

In either kind of instance the customer is seeking help from a medium or diviner. Throughout Scripture God condemns such practitioners and those who frequent them. They claim to speak for God but are actually frauds.

They see falsehood and lying divination who are saying, "The Lord declares," when the Lord has not sent them; yet they hope for the fulfillment of their word. Did you not see a false vision and speak a lying divination when you said, "The Lord declares," but it is not I who have spoken? Therefore, says the Lord God, "Because you have spoken falsehood and seen a lie, therefore behold, I am against you," declares the Lord God (Ezekiel 13:6-9, NASB).

Psychometry

Psychometry can also be classed in the area of fortunetelling. The idea behind psychometry is summed up in the *Dictionary of Mysticism:*

> The psychic faculty of certain persons to divine events connected with material objects when in close contact with the latter. The material objects are considered to be acting as catalysts for the PSI faculty. Occultists call it "reading or seeing" with the inner sight (Frank Gaynor, ed., *Dictionary of Mysticism*, New York: Citadel Press, n.d., p. 148).

Psychometry consists of a person holding some material object of another in his hands and having the ability to make statements and identify characteristics of the owner of the article. He may even foretell part of the future of the owner.

Psychometry has no place in the Christian's life. We are not to depend on mediums and their paraphernalia for help in this world. Rather than depending on other men who are fallible and serving Satan rather than the Lord God, we should depend on the Holy Spirit, whose specific job is to guide us in God's will. Christians can avail themselves of the only true "medium," the Holy Spirit.

> And I will ask the Father, and He will give you another Helper, that He may be with you forever; that is the Spirit of Truth, whom the world cannot receive, because it does not behold Him or know Him... (John 14:16, 17, NASB).
>
> But the Helper, the Holy Spirit, whom the Father will send in My name, He will teach you all things, and bring to your remembrance all that I said unto you (John 14:26, NASB).
>
> And in the same way the Spirit also helps our weaknesses; for we do not know how to pray as we should, but the Spirit Himself intercedes for us with groanings too deep for words; and He who searches the hearts knows what the mind of the Spirit is, because He intercedes for the saints according to the will of God (Romans 8:26, 27, NASB).

We have no need of psychometry or any other occultic practice if we have the Holy Spirit within us.

There are other types of fortunetelling which include:

> *Teacup Reading*—This form of divination interprets the shapes and relative positions left by tea leaves at the bottom of a cup. Fortunes are told using the same principles as are found in the oriental I CHING readings.
>
> *Geomancy*—This system of divination employs a map with

12 divisions in which the symbols of geomancy are placed in conjunction with the planets.

Pyromancy — Divination by use of fire configurations.

Aeromancy — This form of divination observes atmospheric conditions or ripples on the surface of an open body of water.

Arithmancy — Divination by numbers, especially by attaching mystical significance to the numbers associated with a person, especially those numbers associated with the letters of the person's name.

Augury — "In ancient Rome, divination by the flight of birds. The word is used generally for all kinds of divination, also for any omen or sign on which divination is or can be based" (Frank Gaynor, op. cit., p. 21).

Capnomancy — This form of divination uses the smoke of an altar or sacrificial incense as a means of foretelling the future.

Rhapsodamancy — This form of divination is based upon a line in a sacred book that strikes the eye when the book is opened after the diviner prays, meditates or invokes the help of spirits.

In conclusion, there are many different names for fortunetellers or mediums. By whatever name, they are completely condemned by the Bible. God calls them detestable in Deuteronomy 18:11, 12. One who practices such things was condemned to death under the Old Testament theocracy (Leviticus 20:6, 27).

Such false prophets (Jeremiah 14:14) were sometimes called astrologers (Isaiah 47:13), mediums (Deuteronomy 18:11), diviners (Deuteronomy 18:14), magicians (Genesis 41:8), soothsayers (Isaiah 2:6), sorcerers (Acts 13: 6, 8), and spiritists (Deuteronomy 18:11).

The Lord God promises that someday he will "cut off sorceries from your hand, and you will have fortunetellers no more" (Micah 5:12).

CHAPTER ELEVEN

Ghosts

G hosts are said to be spirit apparitions through which the souls of dead persons are said to manifest themselves. All of us have heard fictionalized "ghost stories" from the time we were children. While we dismiss such stories now as figments of fertile juvenile imaginations, we cannot altogether dismiss the whole idea of genuine spirit phenomena popularly associated with ghosts, sometimes called poltergeists.

There are thousands of sophisticated, intelligent people around the world who are convinced that ghosts not only exist, but they can and do communicate with the living.

Are there actually supernatural spirit phenomena associated in a way so as to be labeled poltergeist activity? And if there are, are they adequately explained as the spirits of the deceased?

Milbourne Cristopher, known as America's foremost magician, was also a psychic researcher. Cristopher was convinced that the accounts of ghosts and haunted houses could be explained on a natural level. He offers the following account of a so-called haunted house that was found to have a natural explanation:

> There are sounds in old houses that are not made by human hands or human voices. They are heard during storms or at certain seasons of the year or in some cases on specific days and at specific times. When the sounds persist, rumors spread that houses are haunted, and they are difficult to sell or rent.

An undated clipping, preserved by Houdini, reports such a story. In Union, New York, seven miles from Binghamtom, a once attractive two-story cottage was deteriorating. Paint peeled and cracked from its clapboards, grime clouded its remaining windows. Hinges, long unoiled, creaked, and the floors squeaked if a youngster, intrigued by the empty building, forced open a door and ran through the rooms. The neglected frame cottage was owned by J. W. McAdam of New York City. For two and a half years a man named Hakes had rented it. Neither he, his wife, nor his two children noticed anything peculiar during their occupancy.

Edgar Williams was the next tenant. He and his wife were the first to report that something unusual was taking place. It did not happen often, Williams told the real estate agent, but whenever a high wind swept across the property, bending the branches of trees, a wailing cry would echo through the upper floor. It was impossible to sleep then, he went on; his wife became so agitated that he thought her terror might affect her mind.

The agent went through the house, but could find nothing that might produce the weird sound. Shortly after this, the Williamses moved out. The next tenant had not been told of the strange noise. Less than a month later, he too was in to see the real estate man. He asked if anything odd had ever happened in the house. A murder, perhaps? The agent assured him that to the best of his knowledge nothing of this nature had ever taken place within the four walls. Then the tenant admitted that his wife too had heard the shrill shriek in the night; she thought it came from the garret. The agent made another trip to the house. This time he thoroughly examined the garret on the pretext that the roof might need repair. Again his search for a clue to the mystery was unsuccessful. In less than a week the house was vacant.

Three more families lived briefly in the cottage, all heard the strange, wailing cries. By now the story had spread through the area. It was impossible to rent the haunted house. Uncared for, it gradually took on an appearance that only a ghost would relish.

Early in December a man visited the real estate office and asked if the place which he had heard was haunted could be rented for a short period. The agent, delighted that interest was being expressed in a piece of property he had thought would never produce another penny, answered warily, Yes, the house was available, but as to the haunting stories, they were sheer nonsense. The stranger put him straight. He was interested in a haunted house; he was investigating spiritualism and would like a week to study the sounds the people in that part of the state attributed to a ghost. The agency gave him access to the cottage for seven days without charge. When the man returned to the real estate office again, the rental agent was expecting the same old story of cries in the night. He asked: "Have you laid the ghost?" His visitor replied: "I have, and here it is." The man reached in his pocket and took out a small metal object he had found in the garret. He displayed it on the palm of his hand. It was a toy—a child's whistle, sound, with a hole in the side.

"This had been fastened in a knothole," he said, "and was directly opposite a broken pane of glass. When the wind blew hard, it caused a draft, and the wild shrieks your tenants heard were the natural result."

Who would have guessed that one of the Hakes children, while playing in the garret, had plugged a hole with the whistle, or that a blast of wind would make it sound? Yet there are many accounts of how strange sounds in old houses have been made in the past. The whistle in Union, New York, was something new, but currents of air have accounted for other mysterious noises throughout the years (Milbourne Cristopher, *ESP, Seers And Psychics*, New York: Thomas Crowell Co., 1970, pp. 167-169).

While many such phenomena can be explained easily in natural terms, especially by means of deception, fraud and/or trickery, some poltergeist activity seems to defy natural explanation.

Allen Spraggett records the following ghost story:

Believe in ghosts? If not, how would you explain this true story?

One winter night, in northern Ontario, Canada, during the early days of World War Two, a middle-aged widow awakened from a troubled sleep to see her younger brother standing at the foot of her bed.

The eerie thing was that the woman knew her brother was in England serving with the Royal Canadian Air Force.

Yet she saw him clearly, dressed in his pilot's flying suit, his face deathly pale and solemn beyond description. The effect was horrific. The woman screamed. Abruptly the strange phantasm vanished.

When the woman's three teen-aged children rushed into the room, they found her sobbing, "He's dead, I know he's dead."

The premonition proved to be correct. Sometime later, word came that the brother's Spitfire had been shot down over the English Channel on the same day—possibly at the same hour—that the woman saw the spectral figure in her room.

This story was told to me by one of those intimately involved—the woman's son, who was a member of a church of which I was pastor (Allen Spraggett, *The Unexplained*, New York: Signet Mystic Books, 1967, p. 13).

In his excellent and extremely well-documented book, *Can We Explain the Poltergeist?* A. R. G. Owen gives some examples of genuine poltergeist (ghostly) activity. One case in particular which convinced him poltergeist activity does exist happened in Sauchie, Scotland, in 1960.

Owen goes into great detail (more than 40 pages) of the phenomena of Sauchie, which included the production of noises (tappings, knockings, sawings, bumpings) and the movement of objects. His learned conclusions were as follows:

"It is convenient to say at the outset that the evidence presented is to my mind conclusive proof of the objective reality of two types of poltergeist phenomena: production of noises...movement of objects...In my opinion the Sauchie case must be regarded as establishing beyond all reasonable doubt the objective reality of some poltergeist phenomena" (A. R. G. Owen, *Can We Explain the Poltergeist?*, New York: Garret Pubns.-Helix Press, 1964, pp. 130, 169).

Examining this case of ghostly apparitions, we as Christians can use Scriptural principles to define our Christian response to such spirit phenomena.

Remember, much of what is reported as ghostly or spirit phenomena is fraudulent. It is either deliberately manufactured "evidence," or a natural explanation for the phenomena is more reasonable and probable than a supernatural explanation. We are not concerned here with such natural phenomena, but only with that which defies natural explanation.

Whatever supernatural appearance is involved in ghostly appearances, they are not the appearance of the souls or spirits of persons who are now dead. The Bible assures us that Christians who die go *immediately* to be with the Lord Jesus Christ (2 Corinthians 5:1-9; Philippians 1:21-25).

Non-Christians, on the other hand, go immediately to

Hades, the spirit abode of the dead. There is active punishment for the unredeemed in Hades and no allowance is made for the dead to visit the land of the living no matter how briefly. In fact, in Luke 16:19-31, Jesus Christ presented us with the story of a non-believer who died and desired to send dead Lazarus back to the land of the living to warn his still living brothers not to reject the truth as he had done.

"But Abraham said, 'They have Moses and the prophets; let them hear them.' But he said, 'No, father Abraham, but if someone goes to them from the dead, they will repent!' But he said to him, 'If they do not listen to Moses and the prophets, neither will they be persuaded if someone rises from the dead'" (Luke 16:29-31, NASB). As a matter of fact, Jesus Christ the "firstborn from the dead" (Colossians 1:18) conquered death and was resurrected and many people still don't believe his message of good news and eternal life!

A common denominator in the most convincing ghost stories we hear is that the ghosts don't have peace. They are in some sort of torment, usually bound in some way to the place or building where they died. As we have already seen, the spirit of a Christian would go immediately to be with Jesus Christ. He would not be without peace.

In fact, the Bible promises that for the Christian, "You have not received a spirit of slavery leading to fear again, but you have received a spirit of adoption..." (Romans 8:15, NASB). While it is true that the non-Christian soul has no peace, his unrest is not because of what is going on in our world, but because of the torment he suffers in Hades as a direct result of his willful rejection of free salvation offered by Jesus Christ (Luke 16:23; 2 Peter 2:1).

Common ghost stories center on the departed spirit's compulsion to see his murder avenged. He cannot rest, it is said, until the crime is punished. This desire for personal vengeance, exemplified by such "hauntings," is denied to one who desires to follow the Lord. "Never take your own revenge, beloved, but leave room for the wrath of God, for it is written, 'Vengeance is mine, I will repay,' says the Lord" (Romans 12:19, NASB).

We know of no instance when a supposed ghost preached the truth of the living God. Galatians 1:8-10 warns us not to accept anyone, even an angel, who brings a gospel contrary to that revealed in God's Word. There is no need for a Christian's spirit to return to "haunt" this world. Jesus Christ conquered death and rose from the dead to prove the good news of God's love and grace extended to mankind. Surely His Word is of more value than that of a disembodied spirit!

The spirit of a non-Christian is not permitted to leave its place of torment in Hades and even if it could, it would not bring the gospel of our Lord and Master. We must reject all such messages.

We believe that the ghost experiences that defy natural explanation are demonic in origin. Hebrews 2:14 notes Satan's preoccupation with death. It would be fitting for his legions to pretend to be the spirits of the departed. The Bible even tells of a demon-possessed man who had a compulsion to roam a graveyard (Matthew 8:28; Mark 5:2-5).

Christians have no need to fear death. Jesus Christ conquered death that He "might deliver those who through fear of death were subject to slavery all their lives" (Hebrews 2:15, NASB).

CHAPTER TWELVE

Hypnotism

D r. Nandor Fodor defines hypnotism as "a peculiar state of consciousness, artificially induced, which liberates subconscious powers in the subject, puts him in rapport with the hypnotizer, makes him accept and meticulously execute any of his suggestions, whether hypnotic or post-hypnotic, which do not conflict with deeper instincts of self-preservation and morality, and produces such strange physiological effects as anesthesia and the remarkable control over organic processes of the body. In hypnotic sleep the waking stimuli are strongly resisted, the sleeper hears and answers" (Nandor Fodor, *Encyclopedia of Psychic Science*, Secaucus, NJ: University Books, 1966, p. 77).

An objective, non-psychically oriented definition of hypnosis is "a sleeplike state that nevertheless permits a wide range of behavioral responses to stimulation. The hypnotized individual appears to heed only the communications of the hypnotist.... Even memory and awareness of self may be altered by suggestion, and the effects of the suggestions may be extended (post-hypnotically) into subsequent waking activity" (*Encyclopedia Britannica*, Chicago: Encyclopedia Britannica Publishers, 1974, Macropaedia, Vol. 9, p. 133).

Hypnotism could then be defined as a means of bringing on an artificial state of sleep or reduced consciousness.

Hypnotism is used in a variety of ways. There are those

who practice self-hypnosis who attempt to rid themselves of some bad habit or to put their mind in a more restful state. Some religionists practice extreme methods of self-hypnosis in an attempt to make themselves insensitive to the pain of sticking knives through various parts of their body. Some magicians use hypnosis as a means of entertaining the public. It is not unusual for schools to allow magic shows where the magician will call up several students in order to hypnotize them.

Many physicians use hypnosis for diagnosis and therapy in treating illnesses. The idea is to alter negative aspects of a person's behavior. Another use of hypnotism, which is much too common, is the occultist who uses hypnotism as a magic art to control the behavior of individuals.

There is a wide difference of opinion on the validity and usefulness of hypnotism. Some see hypnotism as being neutral, neither good nor bad, while others argue that hypnotism can be beneficial for diagnosis and therapy. There are yet others who see hypnotism as harmful, no matter what the case, because it is an attack on the human psyche.

Although some physicians do use hypnosis for treating certain illnesses, there is a great degree of association between hypnosis and occultism. Moreover, there are those engaged in hypnosis who have little or no training either medically or psychiatrically who use hypnosis for entertainment purposes. Both the occultic and the unprofessional use of hypnosis can have disastrous effects. Consider the following example from Kurt Koch:

> I was asked to speak at several meetings in a Baptist church in the state of Maine. The pastor of the church told me the story of his son while I was there.
>
> His son had been converted to Christ at the age of sixteen. He was baptized and became a member of his father's church. He went to college about sixty miles from his hometown.
>
> At the end of the college year, an entertainment was held for the students and teachers. The president invited a certain entertainer who performed all kinds of tricks and illusions. One thing he did was to pick out twenty-five students and bring them up to the platform to be hypnotized. One of them was given a big red potato, and it was suggested to him that it was a wonderful apple which he was now allowed to eat. The boy ate the red potato with great delight. To another boy, the

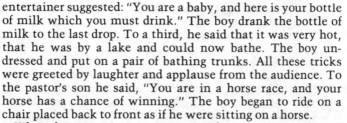

entertainer suggested: "You are a baby, and here is your bottle of milk which you must drink." The boy drank the bottle of milk to the last drop. To a third, he said that it was very hot, that he was by a lake and could now bathe. The boy undressed and put on a pair of bathing trunks. All these tricks were greeted by laughter and applause from the audience. To the pastor's son he said, "You are in a horse race, and your horse has a chance of winning." The boy began to ride on a chair placed back to front as if he were sitting on a horse.

When the entertainment was over, the entertainer released them from the hypnosis; all except the pastor's son, whom he could not restore to consciousness. The president became angry. But try as he might, the man was unable to bring him back from this hypnotic state. There was nothing to do but to call the hospital.

An ambulance took the boy to the hospital where five specialists tried to deal with the hypnotized boy. They were unable to. The father was not informed until six days later. He drove straight to the hospital by car and took his son home. Then he remembered his local doctor who came immediately. The doctor was angry and said, "If he were my son, I would take the principal and the entertainer to court." The pastor and his wife prayed for days, but nothing happened. Suddenly, the pastor came upon the idea of commanding in the name of Jesus. He looked in spirit to the cross of Christ on Calvary and cried: "In the name of Jesus Christ, the Son of God, I command you dark powers to withdraw." At once the hypnotic spell was broken. The boy regained consciousness. At last the horse race ended (Kurt Koch, *Occult ABC*, Grand Rapids, MI: Int. Publs., n.d., pp. 97, 98).

Since there are so many examples of hypnosis which have ended in disaster, we would strongly warn people to stay away from all forms of either occultic or entertaining hypnosis. If a person allows himself to be hypnotized, it should be only under the most controlled situation by a qualified and experienced physician. The human mind is not something to play with or to let another person have control of. At best, hypnosis can have only limited use.

Even the secular *Encyclopedia Britannica* warns:

> While little skill is required to induce hypnosis, considerable training is needed to evaluate whether it is the appropriate treatment technique and, if so, how it should properly be employed. When used in the treatment context, hypnosis should never be employed by individuals who do not have the

competence and skill to treat such problems without the use of hypnosis. For this reason hypnosis "schools" or "institutions" cannot provide the needed training for individuals lacking the more general scientific and technical qualifications of the healing professions.... Improperly used, hypnosis may add to the patient's psychiatric or medical difficulties. Thus, a sufferer of an undiscovered brain tumor may sacrifice his life in the hands of a practitioner who successfully relieves his headache by hypnotic suggestion, thereby delaying needed surgery. Broad diagnostic training and therapeutic skill are indispensable in avoiding the inappropriate and potentially dangerous use of hypnosis (*Encyclopedia Britannica*, op. cit., p. 139).

The Bible says, "All things are lawful for me, but not all things are profitable. All things are lawful for me, but I will not be mastered by anything" (1 Corinthians 6:12, NASB). We do not need to be mastered by the power of suggestion from another.

CHAPTER THIRTEEN

Magic

When we speak of magic, we are dealing with a term having a variety of meanings. People use the expression, "It's magic!" when they see something incredible. We also speak of magic being in the air when there is a particularly pleasant mood.

One of the popular uses of the word magic is in the field of show business. Magic shows entertain us when the magician saws someone in half or pulls a rabbit out of his hat. This type of magic is called sleight of hand or, as the French term it, *legerdemain*. It is the art of illusion.

Certain primitive people have a magical view of life with customs and practices based upon sheer superstition. They consider certain phenomena magic because they have not learned the natural explanation of the occurrence (for example, an eclipse of the sun).

However, the magic we are concerned with is none of the above. It is occultic in nature, an attempt to master supernormal forces in order to produce visible effects. This magic is a secretive art, and it is difficult to give a precise definition of all it includes.

Arthur S. Gregor defines magic in the following manner: "Magic is an attempt to gain control over nature by supernatural means. It consists of spells, charms, and other techniques intended to give man what he cannot achieve with his normal human powers" (Arthur S. Gregor, *Witchcraft and Magic*, New York: Charles Scribner's Sons, 1972, p. 1).

Magic, used mainly by witches, is described by Truzzi:

> For some witchcraft practitioners, especially the more or-
> thodox or traditional ones, magic is viewed as a supernatural
> phenomenon. The character of magic is such that it involves
> special spiritual agencies (e.g., elementals, demons, etc.)
> which are outside the natural physical order available for
> study by empirical science. Thus, for some witches, magical
> laws are not natural laws, and they can even contradict
> natural laws. Supernatural agencies and mechanisms are
> invoked, and these are beyond scientific explanation (Mar-
> cello Truzzi, "Toward a Sociology of the Occult: Notes on
> Modern Witchcraft" in *Religious Movements in Con-
> temporary America*. Irving I. Zaretsky and Mark P. Leone,
> eds., Princeton: Princeton University Press, 1974, p. 635).

There are different types of magic practiced today.
These include:

White Magic

White magic is said to be the use of magical powers and
abilities in an unselfish manner for the benefit of others. It
is believed a person could be cured of bewitchment by
white magic. "If a child is bewitched, we take the
cradle... throw it three times through an enchanted hoop,
ring or belt, and then a dog throws it; and then shakes the
belt over the fire... and then throws it down on the ground
till a dog or cat goes over it, so that the sickness may leave
the sick person and enter the dog or cat" (R. Seth, *In the
Name of the Devil*, 1969).

A witch in seventeenth-century Scotland described how
white magic could be used to cure sickness:

> "When we wished to heal any sore, or broken limb, we would
> say three times:
>
>> He put the blood to the blood, till all up stood;
>> The lith to the lith, till all took with;
>> Our Lady charmed her darling son,
>> With her tooth and her tongue
>> And her ten fingers
>> In the name of the Father, The Son and The Holy Ghost.
>
> And this we say three times stroking the sore, and it becomes
> whole. (Roger Hart, *Witchcraft*, New York: G. P. Putnam's
> Sons, 1971).

Although white magic was and is used to combat evil, it

still comes from an ungodly source and should in no way
be practiced.

Black Magic

The opposite of white magic is the familiar black magic
which can be defined as the use of magical powers to cause
harm to others.

Sympathetic Magic

Sympathetic magic can be defined in the following
manner:

> Control of a person, animal, object, or event by either of two
> principles: 1) Like produces like — for example, a drawing of a
> deer pierced by arrows supposedly would help a tribe's real
> hunters repeat the scene. 2) Things that were once in contact
> always retain a magic connection — for example, a man
> supposedly could be harmed if a lost tooth fell into enemy
> hands (Daniel Cohen, *Superstition*, Mankato, MN: Creative
> Education Society, 1971, p. 115).

Sympathetic magic is based upon the principle of "like
produces like"; that is, things having a resemblance to
each other in shape have a magical relationship.

Liturgy of Magic

Often the rituals of magic are similar to the Christian
faith. Merrill Unger compares magic liturgy and Christian
worship:

> A magic ceremony commonly involves the use of four
> elements — invocation, charm, symbolic action, and a fetish.
> In the case of white magic, the invocation is addressed to God
> the Father, God the Son, and God the Holy Spirit. If black
> magic is involved, the invocation is addressed to Satan and
> demonic powers. Such invocation is the counterpart of
> calling upon God through the Lord Jesus Christ. The in-
> vocation of black magic is commonly fortified by a pact with
> Satan in which the person signs himself over to the devil with
> his own blood.
> The charm, which conjures the magic powers into
> operation, is the counterpart of the Word of God and prayer
> The symbolic action, which is multifarious, mimics biblical
> symbolic action such as forms of prayer or imposition of
> hands in prayer.

Examples of charms taken from *The Sixth and Seventh Books of Moses* are (1) the transference charm of black magic. Boil the flesh of a swine in the urine of an ailing person, then feed this concoction to a dog. As the dog dies, the ailing person will recover. (2) A healing charm of white magic. Eat, unread, some walnut leaves inscribed with a Bible text. (3) A fertility charm of white magic. Place a woman's hair between two loaves of bread and feed this to cattle while saying a magic verse.

Magical symbolism and fetish. Magic symbolism is intended to give effectiveness to the magic charm and bring about occult transference. Magic symbolism, in turn, is supported by a fetish. This is a magically charmed object which is supposed to carry magical power. Any object, of the most bizarre character, can become a fetish by being magically charmed. The magical effectiveness of the fetish (amulet or talisman) is increased by inscriptions, particularly by magic charm formulas (Merrill Unger, *Demons in the World Today*, Wheaton, IL: Tyndale House Publishers, 1971, pp. 90, 91).

Lycanthropy

Lycanthropy is a form of magic which believes human beings under certain conditions can change into animals. The most well-known form of lycanthropy is: a man can change himself either permanently or temporarily into a werewolf. The following 16th century Baltic tale gives an example of this transformation:

At Christmas, a crippled boy goes around the country summoning the devil's followers, who are countless, to a general meeting. Whoever stays behind, or goes unwillingly, is beaten by another with an iron whip till the blood flows, and his traces are left in blood.

The human form vanishes, and the whole multitude become werewolves. Many thousands assemble. Foremost goes the leader armed with an iron whip, and the troop follow, firmly convinced in their imagination that they are transformed into wolves. They fall upon herds of cattle and flocks of sheep, but they have no power to slay men. When they come to a river, the leader strikes the water with his scourge, and it divides, leaving a dry path through the oidst, by which the pack go. The transformation lasts twelve days. At the end of this time the wolf skin vanishes, and the human form reappears.

Although lycanthropy is considered mere legend and superstition, there have been modern reports of this phenomena occurring. The following case is cited by John Warwick Montgomery in his book, *Principalities and Powers*, wherein he is quoting from Frederick Kaigh, who alleges his statement to be based upon eyewitness testimony:

Now from the distance, out of the bush, came jackal cries, nearer and nearer. The deep growl of the male being answered by the shriller cries of the female.

Suddenly a powerful young man and a splendid young girl, completely naked, leapt over the heads of the onlookers and fell sprawling in the clearing.

They sprang up again instantly and started to dance. My God, how they danced! If the dance of the nyanga (the witch doctor) was horrible, this was revolting. They danced the dance of the rutting jackals. As the dance progressed, their imitations became more and more animal, till the horror of it brought the acid of vomit to the throat. Then, in a twinkling, with loathing unbounded, and incredulous amazement, I saw these two *turn into jackals before my eyes*. The rest of their "act" must be rather imagined than described. Suffice it to say, and I say it with all the authority of long practice of my profession (medicine), no human beings, despite any extensive and potent preparation, could have sustained the continued and repeated sexuality of that horrid mating (Frederick Kaigh, *Witchcraft and Magic of Africa*, London: Richard Lesley, 1947, p. 32).

A summary view of the two main types of magic:

This has led to a common distinction made by occultists between so-called *black* and *white* magic. In part the view on this issue depends upon the witch's relation to Christianity. For a pure Satanist, the magic he practices is black in that its power supposedly derives from the forces of evil and darkness (though he may regard Christian miracles like transubstantiation to be instances of white magic). But for the witch who has no belief in the Christian's hell or devil, magic derives from special laws in nature. Because of the common public sterotype of the witch as Satanist, however, many non-Christian witches began to speak of themselves as *white witches* and began referring to magic they did as white or beneficial. But this reference to white and black magic was meant to refer to the intentions of the magician in its invocation, not to the character of the magic itself (Truzzi, *Religious Movements*, op. cit., p. 635).

CHAPTER FOURTEEN

Ouija Boards

One of the most popular occultic devices in the world today is the Ouija board. What is the Ouija board and what does it claim to do? *The Dictionary of Mysticism* has this to say concerning the Ouija board:

> An instrument for communication with the spirits of the dead. Made in various shapes and designs, some of them used in the sixth century before Christ. The common feature of all its varieties is that an object moves under the hand of the medium, and one of its corners, or a pointer attached to it, spells out messages by successively pointing to letters of the alphabet marked on a board which is a part of the instrument (Frank Gaynor, ed., *Dictionary of Mysticism*, New York: Citadel Press, n.d., p. 132).

The Ouija board is considered by some as nothing more than a party game. Others believe that using it can reveal hidden things in the subconscious. Still others believe that, while the communications are produced supernaturally, the supernatural source is demonic rather than from "beyond the grave." One Christian authority on the occult, Kurt Koch, has strong feelings on the subject:

> ...psychologists would have us believe that the game is harmless. They hold that it is only a matter of bringing to light things hidden in our subconscious minds. This view can swiftly be refuted. With the Ouija board, revelations from the hidden past and predictions about the future are made. These things could not possibly be stored in our subconscious

minds (Kurt Koch, *Occult ABC*, Grand Rapids, MI: Int. Publs., n.d., p. 152).

Our convictions concerning the Ouija board agree exactly with those of noted cult and occult observer Edmond Gruss.

The Ouija board should be seen as a device which sometimes actually makes contact with the supernatural for several reasons:

— The content of the messages often goes beyond that which can be reasonably explained as coming from the conscious or subconscious mind of the operator. Examples of such are presented in Sir William F. Barrett's *On the Threshold of the Unseen* (pp. 176-189), and in the experiences of Mrs. John H. Curran, related in the book *Singer in the Shadows*.

— The many cases of "possession" after a period of Ouija board use also support the claim that supernatural contact is made through the board. Psychics and parapsychologists have received letters from hundreds of people who have experienced "possession" (an invasion of their personalities). Rev. Donald Page, a well-known clairvoyant and exorcist of the Christian Spiritualist Church, is reported as saying that most of his "possession" cases "are people who have used the Ouija board," and that "this is one of the easiest and quickest ways to become possessed" (*Man, Myth and Magic*, number 73, after p. 2060). While Page views these "possessions" as caused by disincarnate entities, the reality of possession is still clear. The Christian sees the invader as an evil spirit (demon).

— The board has been subjected to tests which support supernatural intervention. The testing of the board was presented in an article by Sir William Barrett, in the September 1914 *Proceedings of the American Society for Psychical Research* (pp. 381-894). The Barrett report indicated that the board worked efficiently with the operators blindfolded, the board's alphabet rearranged and its surface hidden from the sight of those working it. It worked with such speed and accuracy under these tests that Barrett concluded:

> Reviewing the results as a whole I am convinced of their supernormal character, and that we have here an exhibition of some intelligent, disincarnate agency, mingling with the personality of one or more of the sitters and guiding their muscular movements (p. 394).

In his book, *On the Threshold of the Unseen*, Barrett

referred to these same experiences and stated: "...Whatever may have been the source of the intelligence displayed, it was absolutely beyond the range of any normal human faculty" (p. 181). Similar statements could be multiplied.

The fact remains that the Ouija board works. Much phenomena is certainly through conscious and sub-conscious activity, but that some is of supernatural character must be accepted (Edmond Gruss, *Cults and Occult in the Age of Aquarius*, Phillipsburg, NJ: 1980, pp. 115, 116).

The magician, Danny Korem, feels there is nothing supernatural connected with the Ouija board.

I have never witnessed, read, or heard of a credible report of something of a supernatural nature taking place through the use of the Ouija board. I have seen, heard, and read, however, of many negative experiences that have entrapped people who have sought knowledge with a Ouija board. If you own a Ouija board or some similar diversion, my advice is to destroy it and never encourage others to tinker with such devices. You never know what emotional disturbances might be triggered in yourself or others through their use.

If you are still unconvinced and believe that some power might be manifested, then one should utilize the following procedure. The letters should be scattered at random, without your knowledge of their position, around the board; a bag should be placed over your head to prevent your viewing the board; and the entire letter-finding task should be viewed by a qualified magician, who would verify your lack of vision. Then and only then, if there are forces at work, will they produce something literate let alone prophetic. To save you the time and effort, let me add that this has already been tried with negative results (Danny Korem and Paul Meier, *The Fakers*, Grand Rapids, MI: Baker Book House, 1980, pp. 70, 71).

The Ouija board is not a plaything. It is another tool often used by Satan to get people to look somewhere else besides to Jesus Christ for the answers. Whether super-natural forces are at work or not, if the person using the Ouija board thinks the supernatural is at work, he will then employ it rather than looking to God for ultimate answers.

CHAPTER FIFTEEN

Parapsychology

While the occult generally refers to the darker side of supernatural activity, it now also involves the new discipline of parapsychology.

Parapsychology is a new branch of either the occult or psychology depending on whom you consult. It is a discipline that has aimed to put many of the supernatural phenomena associated with the occult on sound scientific footing. The attempt is to create respectability for what has been considered as foolishness.

One of the popular areas in parapsychology in recent years has been ESP (extra-sensory perception). Traditional witchcraft, which assents to the supernatural, has also given way in some groups to this new scientific or paranormal explanation of occultic activity.

Most newer witchcraft groups, however, avoid supernaturalism and prefer instead to speak of *supernormal* or *paranormal* events. Magical laws are seen as effective and within the ultimate purview of scientific understanding, but their emphasis is placed upon pragmatic knowledge of such magical laws and not on their scientific validation or understanding. In this sense, it would appear that there has been a kind of secularization of magic in adaptation to the modern scientific and naturalistic world view. Thus, what were once described in the occult literature as supernatural psychic forces are now examples of extra-sensory perception of a kind basically examinable and potentially understandable in the psychologist's laboratory (Marcello Truzzi, "Toward a

100

Sociology of the Occult: Notes on Modern Witchcraft,"
Religious Movements in Contemporary America. Irving I.
Zaretsky and Mark P. Leone, eds., Princeton: Princeton
University Press, 1974, pp. 635, 636).

In his book, *Parapsychology: An Insider's View of ESP*,
J. Gaither Pratt, in the first chapter, "The Benign Revolution," points to a new revolution in thought, what he calls
an advance in ideas, the attempt of parapsychology to gain
respectability. He plots his own odyssey, how he came to
embrace this revolution and the need to see parapsychology as a branch of science.
Pratt comments:

> And so this book is about a revolution of human thought. Our
> Western culture has passed through a number of great
> changes in ways of thinking since the Renaissance, others are
> in the process of taking place, and many more will un-
> doubtedly come in the years and centuries ahead. The ad-
> vance in thinking with which this book is concerned is still
> in the process of taking shape. Indeed, it is even still in a very
> early stage of development, though not too early to be
> recognized and to be appreciated for what it has already ac-
> complished as well as for its far greater potentialities yet to be
> appreciated.
>   This is the revolution of thinking embodied in the new
> branch of science, parapsychology. The definition of this field
> is quite simple: as physics is the science which deals with
> matter, so parapsychology is the science of mind. So simple
> to state, yet so far-reaching in its implications! It will be the
> main task of this book to present some highlights of past
> accomplishments in this field and the general scope and
> direction of present efforts—and to explore and explain the
> meaning of its findings (J. Gaither Pratt, *Parapsychology: An
> Insider's View of ESP*, New York: Doubleday & Co., 1964,
> pp. 2, 3).

For men such as Pratt, parapsychology demands investigation from a scientific perspective. The experiences
which people have should be investigated to determine
just what the possibilities are in this field of the mind.

> Let us return to the main theme of the chapter: what this
> book is about in terms of the meaning, scope, and contents of
> the field itself. Earlier, I ventured to suggest that parapsychol-
> ogy is the science of mind. Parapsychology began when
> scientists frankly faced up to the questions posed by ex-

periences from everyday life suggesting action at a distance without any sort of physical contact. These are experiences which suggest that man may be capable of gaining knowledge of distant or future events when there is no conceivable physical energy reaching any of his sense organs. If these things have any real basis in fact, then something more than the operation of the laws of physics seems to be involved (Ibid, p. 12).

In *Parapsychology and the Nature of Life*, John L. Randall comments:

> As the 1960s drew to a close parapsychology won a substantial victory in its ninety-year-old battle for scientific respectability. On December 30th, 1969, the Parapsychological Association was officially accepted as an affiliate member of that most distinguished body of savants, the American Association for the Advancement of Science (A.A.A.S.). The decision to grant affiliation to the parapsychologists was taken by the A.A.A.S. council, an organization composed of delegates from about 300 other affiliated scientific, medical and engineering societies; so it represented the views of a considerable cross-section of American science. For the first time in its chequered history, parapsychology had been recognized as a legitimate scientific pursuit; and from now on parapsychologists could present their papers at the bar of scientific opinion without feeling that they would be ridiculed or dismissed out of hand merely on account of their subject matter (John L. Randall, *Parapsychology and the Nature of Life*, New York: Harper and Row Publishers, p. 175).

The demand for scientific investigation is a valid quest and should and must be made. This responsibility lies with Christians too. However, in the consideration of parapsychology as science, one must be willing to embrace the most accurate explanation of the data, whether it be fraud, the occult or a valid paranormal experience.

For in most cases, one fruit in the study of parapsychology is an increasing lack of motivation to study the Scriptures. In fact, it often leads one in the directon of the paranormal or supernatural totally apart from a biblical base. In an interesting preface to his book, *Religion and the New Psychology*, Alson J. Smith writes of the story of a young woman he talked to at length doing research in parapsychology at Duke University:

She was a quiet, intelligent girl from the middle South. She had come to Duke intending to go into some kind of religious work; she had been a "local preacher" in her home-town Methodist church and had occupied the pulpit on many occasions. At Duke, however, she had studied the various sciences and had lost most of her old, uncritical religious faith. She gave up the idea of entering religious work and lapsed into a sort of mournful agnosticism.

In the course of her work in psychology, though, she had discovered parapsycholgy, the "venture beyond psychology," with which this book is largely concerned. It was a science in which she had learned to put her trust, and yet it spoke to her of the same spiritual world, the same spiritual forces that her old, uncritical religious faith had spoken of; in a different terminology and by a different method, it came out at the same place. The emotional void left by the loss of her religious faith was filled; her new faith (although I do not think she would call it that) satisfied her intellectually and emotionally. Her laboratory work in parapsychology became for her a sort of religious vocation (Alson J. Smith, *Religion and the New Psychology*, Garden City, NY: Doubleday and Co., Inc., 1951, p. 5).

Smith interestingly enough offers this explanation for the woman's change. He both attributes the demise of her Christian faith and the rise of her "parapsychology faith" to the scientific method:

Her story, it seems to me, is an allegory on what is happening to millions of nominal Christians in our day. Their acceptance of the scientific method has shaken their religious faith (which, of course, has also been shaken by a great many other things), and they are not very happy about it. But they have to accept the scientific method — its accomplishments are too many and too great to be ignored.

The significance of parapsychology for these millions is that it now takes the scientific method and leads men toward the spiritual world rather than away from it. Thus, a synthesis is effected between the old values and the new, authoritative method. The prestige of science is lent to religion, and the humility of true religion is lent to science as it sees that its methods can be used to underline spiritual insights that are as old as the race. Parapsychology, in a word, can make religion intellectually respectable and science emotionally satisfying. And the hope of the world in this time of crisis lies in just such a synthesis as this (Ibid, p. 6).

Not only does this new emphasis on the science of parapsychology affect the way individuals understand Christianity, it also affects the way people understand the Scriptures. Scientists usually accept that similar phenomena occur in both the occult and parapsychology. However, many scientists disagree with the biblical explanation of such phenomena, that it is usually demonic. Often, the new science of parapsychology will discredit any biblical interpretation of the data.

For example, in the book, *Life, Death and Psychical Research: Studies on Behalf of the Churches' Fellowship for Psychical and Spiritual Studies*, the authors discredit the biblical admonition against sorcerers and mediums given in the Book of Deuteronomy. They feel this passage does not prohibit the exercise of psychical (demonic) gifts, the prohibition of which has been the historic and traditional interpretation by the church until the modern attempt to give some type, any type, of biblical credibility to the paranormal.

Consider this:

The Deuteronomic "prohibition" (Deuteronomy 18:9 to 12) has long been used by the prejudiced, the ignorant and the fearful as a reason for opposing genuine psychical research by Christian people. In the past, innocent folk have been denounced as sourcerers and witches or of being possessed by evil spirits. Others, who have exercised powers believed to come under the sacred ban, have been tortured to death.

Such attitudes still persist. Those who seek to exercise psychical gifts are often warned of the dangers of divine condemnation. Christians who encourage paranormal investigation are reminded that they are going against the teachings of the Bible and are forbidden to "dabble" in such matters (Canon J. D. Pearce, Higgens and Rev. Stanley Whitby, eds., *Life, Death and Psychical Research: Studies of the Churches' Fellowship for Psychical and Spiritual Studies*, London: Rider and Company, 1973, p. 10).

While it's true innocent people have been denounced in the past (viz., Salem witch trials), it is a logical fallacy to assume, therefore, that historical interpretation of the Scriptures by Christians on this passage has been wrong, when in fact both history and proper biblical interpretation support their position.

104

ESP

Extra-sensory perception, or ESP as it is commonly known, has become very popular today. To know something without the help of the senses is the meaning of ESP.

Lynn Walker states of ESP:

ESP, or extra-sensory perception... is the term applied to an ability to know something without the aid of the senses. It includes precognition or what is sometimes referred to as "ESP of the future"; telepathy, which is the awareness of the thoughts of a person without the use of the senses; and clairvoyance, the awareness of objects or objective events without sensory aid (Lynn Walker, *Supernatural Power and the Occult*, Austin: Firm Foundation Publishing House, n.d., p. 90).

ESP is only one major field of parapsychology. Another area of study in parapsychology is psychical research:

Systematic scientific inquiries concerning the nature, facts and causes of mediumistic phenomena (Norman Blunsdan, *A Popular Dictionary of Spiritualism*, NY: The Citadel Press, 1963, s.v. "psychical research").

However, what should be noted is that there is a difference between what is often called mental telepathy and ESP. These two often are used interchangeably, but to a parapsychologist they are different.

Mental telepathy is a branch of ESP. In fact, one of the "breakthroughs" in ESP research for parapsychologists was when they made a division between mental telepathy and clairvoyance. In mental telepathy the person is aware of mental images, say symbols on cards, and the cards are shuffled and he tries through ESP to reproduce the images seen.

Clairvoyance, on the other hand, tries to draw the symbols without any prior sense knowledge of what symbols were on the cards (Pratt, op. cit., pp. 45-54). This distinction led to a new emphasis in psychic research. The psychic researchers were able to formulate better test techniques for telepathy, and to determine precisely what was being tested, as well as what might be fraud, and from our perspective what might be strong occultic influence.

Uri Geller

One young Israeli whose name has become synonymous with the respectability of ESP is that of Uri Geller. His appearances and demonstrations around the world have made him famous and have drawn a strong spotlight to the paranormal phenomena. Geller has supposedly demonstrated his capacity to reproduce pictorially items that he cannot see and bend things he cannot touch. Presently Geller is the center of a storm of controversy as to the validity of his claims. Although there has always been disagreement over his abilities, the catalyst for a major foray began after tests conducted at the prestigious Stanford Research Institute. Here is a brief history, beginning with positive testimony from Great Britain:

URI SENDS BRITAIN ON A BIG BENDER, declared a *Sun* headline, while the *News of the World* ran an exclusive, front-page story entitled "Uri's Miracle Pictures," which revealed Uri's ability to take photos of himself with the lens cap still on the camera, with "no signs of trickery." And not only were the newspapers clearly persuaded about Uri's psychic powers, but a number of distintuished scientists and writers were publicly claiming that the "Geller effect" was authentic and scientifically verified.

On the other hand, a number of articles appeared that expressed considerable ambivalence and even outright skepticism about Uri Geller's claims. Barbara Smoker entitled her article, published in the February 1974 issue of the *New Humanist*, "Uri Geller, the Joke's Over!" Smoker took the position that Geller was simply a clever magician.

The June and July 1974 issues of *Psychology Today* contained an interesting account of Geller's abilities by Andrew Weil. Weil was initially convinced by Geller and then disillusioned when Randi (the "Amazing"), a highly talented professional stage magician and escape artist from New Jersey, duplicated all of Geller's effects and more. Andrew Weil ended his two-part article (entitled, "The Letdown") with the conclusion that questions like "Is Uri Geller a fraud?" or "Do psychic phenomena exist?" are unanswerable. "The answer is always yes and no," says Weil, "depending on who is looking and from what point of view."

This skeptical approach to Geller, however, was clearly a minority viewpoint. October 18, 1974, marked the occasion of a unique event in the history of psychic research. One of the world's most respected scientific journals, *Nature*, published an article by Russell Targ and Harold Puthoff of the Stanford Research Institute claiming verification of Geller's ESP ability (David Marks and Richard Kammann, *The Psychology of the Psychic*, Buffalo, New York: Prometheus Books, 1980, p. 74).

Targ and Puthoff had two major experiments. One had Geller draw pictures picked at random by someone else in an isolated room. The second involved Geller's pick of what face on die would be uppermost. Against the odds Geller's accuracy was incredible.

Targ and Puthoff concluded their scientific report with the conclusion that "a channel exists whereby information about a remote location can be obtained by means of an as yet unidentified perceptual modality" — in other words, that ESP is a scientifically proven reality (Ibid, p. 74).

However:

In the same week the *Nature* article appeared, another reputable British journal, *New Scientist*, published a sixteen-page report on Uri Geller by Dr. Joseph Hanlon. Hanlon's thesis was that Geller is a fraud — that he cheats, uses tricks, substitution, distraction, sleight-of-hand and all the other tools of the magician's repertoire (Ibid, p. 75).

In their book, *The Psychology of the Psychic*, the authors Marks and Kammann lay forth a study that bears close scrutiny, where they attempt to show the faulty nature of the Stanford experiments (which have come under a great deal of question by many) and a fraudulent deception on Geller's part. They also attempt to discredit the famous Kreskin, and devote a number of chapters to him as well.

Even with their study, and that of others, one cannot dismiss the work of the Stanford Research Institute lightly, nor some of the feats accomplished by Geller. In all likelihood they appear to be clever magicians' tricks. If not fraud, then possibly Geller has opened himself up to occultic powers to achieve his feats, for Geller certainly does not give credit to the God of the Bible.

University Research

The establishment of university research in the field of parapsychology and psychical study has lent much credibility for its acceptance. Universities such as Stanford and Duke have been instrumental in this regard.

In fact, Duke University has one of the most well-respected facilities for the study of parapsychology. The Duke University Parapsychology Laboratory is located in College Station, Durham, North Carolina. When Duke was founded, the Spiritualist movement was strong in the United States and their claims attracted the attention of the scientific community. Emphasis at that time was on mediumship and telepathy. Dr. J. B. Rhine brought the Laboratory to the prominence it holds today (J. B. Rhine and Associates, *Parapsychology from Duke to FRNM*, Durham, North Carolina: The Parapsychology Press, 1965, pp. 3-28).

Evaluation

How should one evaluate paranormal experiences? One must admit the possibility that such experiences may occur. Dr. J. B. Rhine of Duke University's Parapsychology Laboratory spent a lifetime in an attempt to document the reality of extra-sensory perception.

It can be said that if there is some type of ESP capacity within some individuals, independent of either divine or demonic influence, its moral value would depend on its use. However, there seems to be an unlikelihood of divine use or aid.

The Scriptures have strong language about the use of such powers, where their use is referred to as not being of God. The major emphasis of such ESP experience, as has been shown, generally does not lead one toward biblical truth.

Dr. John Warwick Montgomery, in *Principalities and Powers*, takes a markedly different approach to the reality and experience of ESP than most evangelical scholars. He believes that one should not throw out all the experiences of ESP *a priori* as evil without proper investigation. After his investigation of the evidence Dr. Montgomery contends there may be a type of ESP power associated with individuals in various degrees that is not evil in origin.

Another writer, Lynn Walker, who quotes Dr. Montgomery in *Supernatural Power and the Occult*, also holds to this neutral approach, that simply to admit the existence of the power does not mean to admit evil.

In consideration of Dr. Montgomery's approach, if the power is neutral (neither divine nor demonic) – such as atomic energy is neither good nor evil, for its moral value depends on who uses it and what for (e.g., an atomic bomb dropped to murder the Nazis or a nuclear power plant built to heat a hospital) – then it would seem only limited use would be permitted by God, such as the personal experience of the individual.

For example, when a person suddenly realizes that something evil may happen to a friend or loved one, yet at the moment of realization that friend is clear around the world and he has not seen or spoken to him at all in the recent past and something does happen, then he has had a personal experience that may be best explainable at the present by ESP. But that would be the extent of the "use" by the individual.

That experience or any future experiences would not qualify him to be a prophet, for example. Yet, this limited-use idea does not seem completely consistent with the endowment of other gifts given by God, for all gifts from God (of which ESP thus would be one) are created to be used. Yet instead, here God is placing incredible restrictions on its use.

Of ESP or precognitive ability Dr. John Warwick Montgomery offers these remarks:

> Here we are evidently encountering a mental faculty (analogous to extraordinary vision) which permits some people to look through the temporal haze separating the future from the past....
>
> Where it (precognitive ability) is used as a basis for exaggerated claims in behalf of its possessor – where, for example, the precognitive agent turns himself into, or allows others to turn himself into, a "seer" who can pronounce on the nature of life and the meaning of the universe – precognition becomes a most dangerous quality. Moreover, used in this way, it opens the floodgates of the psyche to supernatural influences of the negative sort (John W. Montgomery, *Principalities and Powers*, Minneapolis, MN: Bethany Fellowship, 1973, pp. 125, 126).

Dr. Montgomery, in his investigation, has completed

some important research that will bear close scrutiny. His work is always thorough.

Lynn Walker sums up the present situation well as he points out that today almost all forms of paranormal activity have no relation to the God of the Bible.

> We must conclude that it is when man, through the influence of Satan's direct power, uses a God-given talent or ability to teach religious error (Colossians 2:8-10; 2 Corinthians 11: 3, 4), to promote works of the flesh (Galatians 5:19f), to exalt self as specially endowed by God as his agent (Colossians 2:18; 2 Corinthians 10:18), to deny the God of the Bible (2 Peter 2:1), to deliberately aspire to go beyond bounds divinely set (Deuteronomy 29:29) – it is then that man has become an instrument of Satan, a tool of evil supernaturalism. Divination in its mulitplied forms and all present-day claims to revelations from God are equally Satan-inspired (Lynn Walker, *Supernatural Power*, op. cit., p. 91).

In summary, except for the unusual experiences reported above, a Christian has no reason to pursue parapsychology. This new discipline does not lead men to God and opens men up to the powers of darkness, just as participation in Mahareshi's Transcendental Meditation (TM) may harm an individual who participates in it.

Lynn Walker in *Supernatural Power and the Occult* explains the options:

> If Satan did not have the power to create an ability in man, then God must have created man with all his abilities and talents; therefore, the ability to be aware of events or thoughts without the aid of the senses, ESP ability, is of God. Just as some men have, for instance, musical talent while others have none or have it in lesser degree, so do some men have ESP ability, some more, some less, some none. Almost everyone studying this lesson knows or has known someone, maybe a relative, who has at some time had a premonition or actually, with even some consistency, anticipated events or read another person's thoughts. To admit such ability does not admit an evil origin. This is not to say, however, that one's ESP ability cannot be misused (Ibid).

CHAPTER SIXTEEN

Psychic Surgery

Psychic surgery is a phenomenon which has gained quite a lot of publicity in recent years. The idea behind psychic surgery is that a psychic can perform miraculous operations on individuals by magic without traditional instruments or techniques and without leaving a scar.

The most famous instances of psychic surgery were performed in recent years by a Brazilian named Arigo, known as "the surgeon with the rusty knife." Arigo was a man with little education and absolutely no medical training. His "operations" were performed while he was in a trance.

He claimed that the actual force behind his incredible operations was a spirit that possessed him. This spirit was supposedly that of a German doctor named Aldolph Fritz, who lived during the turn of the century. His methods, however, were anything but that of a qualified physician. Arigo's operations were performed with a rusty knife without using any anaesthetic or antiseptic.

His procedure included the diagnosis of the patient's disease while Arigo was in a trance. His diagnoses were usually correct. The house in which he performed many of his miracle operations had a sign which read, "Here in this house we are all Catholics." Arigo also would recite the Lord's Prayer before commencing surgery. Obviously, this is not standard operating procedure for surgeons, but the results of this illiterate miner's surgical attempts were amazing.

Kurt Koch lists some of his accomplishments:

I have been to Brazil eight times for various tours. I have also been to Belo Horizonte. In this little town, an incredible surgical miracle was performed by Arigo. Senator Lucio Bittencourt had been holding an election meeting to which Arigo and his friends from Cogonhas had travelled. Bittencourt was suffering from lung cancer and planned to go to the U.S.A. for an operation when the election campaign was over.

The Senator and Arigo were staying at the same hotel. During the night Bittencourt suddenly saw Arigo in his room, with a razor in his hand. He heard Arigo say, "You are in great danger." Then he lost consciousness. When he woke up again, he felt different in himself. He turned the light on and found that there were clots of blood on his pajama jacket. He took the jacket off and looked at his chest in the mirror. On his chest was a fine cut. Knowing what he did of Arigo's healing skills, he hurried to Arigo's room and asked him: "Have you operated on me?"

"No, you must have drunk too much."

"I must know exactly what happened," said the Senator. "I will take the next plane and go to see my doctor in Rio."

Bittencourt told the doctor he had had his operation. The specialist took some x-ray pictures and confirmed it. "Yes. You have been operated on according to American surgical methods. We have not yet gotten so far in Brazil." Then the Senator explained what had taken place. This story caused a great sensation in the papers, and brought a flood of visitors to Arigo's clinic.

American doctors, journalists, and camera men went to Arigo's clinic. They carried out all manner of tests, but were unable to discover any deception. Arigo was willing for any test to be carried out. He even allowed his operations to be filmed. An American doctor, Dr. Puharich, even had a lipoma removed. The operation was performed with a rusty knife, without any local anaesthetic or antiseptic materials. Dr. Puharich felt no pain. This operation was also filmed (Kurt Koch, Occult ABC, Grand Rapids, MI: Int. Publs., n.d., p. 237).

There have been other cases recorded that have not been quite as sensational as Arigo's. Tim Timmons records the following story of a Mexican peasant woman named Carlita. Carlita always operates in a dark room with her eyes closed. Timmons states:

Carlita's healings are strange! She does not pray over a person asking God to heal them—she actually operates on people with a dull hunting knife! Over the past fifty years, she has performed every kind of operation imaginable—on the heart, the back, the eyes, etc. A medical doctor who had observed Carlita perform many operations was present when I interviewed her. He told of one case where Carlita cut into a person's chest cavity, took the heart out for examination and handed it to him. After she closed the person up, without stitches, she suggested that he go to his hotel room and rest for three days. When the three days were up, he left Mexico City, a healthy man, with no scars from surgery. I asked the doctor what explanation he could give for such an amazing work. He replied, "There is no explanation medically. It's a miracle."

However, not everyone sees these as actual accounts of what transpired. Danny Korem says of the Timmons example,

Carlita was very shrewd in having a physician give credence to her powers. Whether he was duped or participated in the sham is unclear. What is amusing is that she only performs her "surgery" in the dark. Of course, with few conjuring techniques at her disposal, how else could she convince her takers that she removed someone's heart with a dull hunting knife! The statement that the wound healed without scarring in three weeks is also easily explained. A slight cutting of the skin where the operation supposedly took place would heal without a scar. The cut actually gave the "surgery" some validity. The apparent healing again cannot be verified as being imaginary or psychosomatic. Is it not obvious why the psychic surgeons couldn't make the first cut for the American Medical Association? (Danny Korem and Paul Meier, *The Fakers*, Grand Rapids, MI: Baker Book House, 1980, pp. 83, 85).

Among psychic investigators there exist differing opinions about the validity of psychic surgery. Kurt Koch comments, "Let us be quite clear about this: Arigo's cures were not a trick or a swindle. They were real operations" (Kurt Koch, *Occult ABC*, op. cit., p. 238). As already stated, there are others who would vehemently disagree with this stance.

It seems difficult to put all psychic surgery in either category, as being all fake or all authentic. Whatever the case may be, it is certainly not a work of God. In the case of Arigo, he would come under the category of an angel of light. His allusions to Jesus and to the Christian religion are covering the fact that he was an instrument of Satan. The idea of being possessed by the spirit of someone else is contrary to the teaching of Scripture and if Arigo was indeed possessed, it was by a demon, not the spirit of a dead German doctor.

Psychic surgery is not the route anyone should dare take, for the spiritual and physical side effects can be fatal. It is much better to take your physical ailments to the Great Physician.

CHAPTER SEVENTEEN

Rosicrucianism

The true origin of Rosicrucianism is unknown. Today there are two groups which claim to be representative of Rosicrucianism and each claims a different origin. The Rosicrucian Fellowship is headquartered in Oceanside, California, and attempts to trace its origin back to the Chaldeans: "The founders of the Rosicrucian system were originally identical with the Chaldeans" (R. Swinburne Clymer, *The Secret Schools*, Oceanside, CA: Philos Publishing, p.16).

The rival organization, the Ancient Mystical Order Rosae Crucis (abbreviated AMORC), headquartered in San Jose, California, dubiously "traces its origin to the mystery schools or secret schools of learning established during the reign of Thutmose III, about 1500 B.C. in Egypt" (*Who and What Are The Rosicrucians?*, p. 8).

This latter group is adamant about being the faithful Rosicrucian order. One of their pamphlets states: "There is but one international Rosicrucian order operating throughout the world...This organization does not sponsor a few modern publishing houses, or book propositions, operating under similar names, or selling instructions or books under the name of Rosicrucian fellowship, society, fraternity and other similar titles" (Anon., *Why Are We Here? And Why Are Our Lives Unequal?*, San Jose, California: The Rosicrucian Press, Ltd., 1952, p. 10).

The earliest authentically Rosicrucian writings come from the 17th century. These are anonymous works entitled *Fama Fraternitatis* and *The Confession of the Order*. These works set forth the travels of the alleged founder of the order, one Christian Rosenkreutz. As the story goes, Rosenkreutz (1378-1484) learned secrets about medicine and magic while on a pilgrimage to the Near East. On his return to Europe, he attempted to share his new knowledge with the world, but his teachings were rejected by the unenlightened public. He then founded a secret fraternity whose members communicated by secret-coded writings.

Upon his death, Rosenkreutz was buried in the house in which the Order met. More than 100 years after his death his grave was opened and, along with his supposed unconsumed body, occultic writings were found. The Order was founded in 1614, based upon the supposed true wisdom and knowledge discovered by Rosenkreutz.

Most scholars agree the story is mythical, but it gives the Order the appearance of historical source. In fact, the author of the Rosenkreutz story later identified himself as Valentine Andreä and then finally admitted that the whole story was fictitious. However, this was not the end of the secret movement:

> Even this disclosure, however, did not prevent many enthusiastic persons from continuing to believe in the reality of Rosicrucian brotherhood, and professing to be acquainted with its secrets (Rev. James Gardner, *The Faiths of the World, Vol. 2*, London: A Fullarton and Co., 1874, p. 775).

What is Rosicrucianism?

The following excerpts from a Rosicrucian writing explains the Rosicrucians' purpose:

> In general terms we may announce that the primary object of Roscrucianism is to elucidate the mysteries that encompass us in life, and reverently to raise the veil from those that await us in the dreaded dominions of death (R. Swinburne Clymer, op. cit., p. 8).

The Rosicrucian Order is syncretistic, meaning that it borrows ideas and beliefs from divergent and sometimes opposing sources, attempting to unify those ideas and beliefs into a coherent world view. Rosicrucians, for all their divergent beliefs, all unify under the central tenet that esoteric wisdom about life beyond the grave has been preserved through the ages and is revealed only to those within the secret brotherhood. Charles Braden observed:

> There are Rosicrucian societies, fraternities, orders, fellowships or lodges in most countries of the modern world. Some of them are very active; others are obscure and highly secret; some seem primarily religious in their emphasis, and some categorically deny that Rosicrucianism is a religion, holding rather that it is a philosophy, making use of the most modern scientific methods and techniques, as well as the methods of the occultist, the mystic and the seer, in the quest for truth.
>
> But, while Rosicrucianism is sectarian in character and the various branches are sometimes bitterly critical of each other, they do have common features, the central one being the purported possession of certain secret wisdom handed down from ancient times, through a secret brotherhood, an esoteric wisdom that can only be imparted to the initiated (Charles Braden, "Rosicrucianism," *Encyclopedia Britannica*, 1964 ed., XIX, p. 558).

The Teachings of Rosicrucianism

Although one of the attractions of Rosicrucianism is its claim that it is not a religion, its writings contain specific religious teaching which denies every cardinal doctrine of Christianity.

The Bible

The Rosicrucian Order does not hold the Bible in any special favor. R. Swinburne Clymer writes, "All secret and sacred writings have truth in them, irrespective of their source, and must be judged by their inculcations rather than the source" (R. Swinburne Clymer, op. cit., p. 19).

Jesus Christ

— "Jesus was born of *Gentile* parents through whose veins flowed Aryan blood" (p. 53).
— Jesus did not die on the cross, for "an examination of the body revealed that Jesus was *not dead*. The blood *flowing from the wounds* proved that His body was not lifeless ...." (p. 265).
— The Ascension is rejected because "there is nothing in the

original accounts of it to warrant the belief that Jesus arose physically or in His physical body in a cloud into the heavens" (p. 283).

— And finally, it is claimed that Rosicrucian archival records "clearly show that after Jesus retired to the monastery at Carmel He lived for many years, and carried on secret missions with His apostles...." (p. 289). (H. Spencer Lewis, *The Mystical Life of Jesus*, 8th ed. 1948).

None of the above claims by the Rosicrucians concerning Jesus Christ conforms to the Bible. Matthew 1:1-18 and Luke 3:23-38 affirm the long Jewish ancestry of the human nature of Jesus Christ. Acts 2:23, 24 clearly shows that the death of Jesus Christ on the cross was according to the predetermined plan of God.

St. Paul reminds us that "if Christ has not been raised, your faith is worthless; you are still in your sins" (1 Corinthians 15:17, NASB). Finally, Acts 1:9-11 and Matthew 24:30 confirm Christ's ascension into heaven and His eventual public (not secret) return to earth. The Jesus Christ of the Rosicrucians is not the Jesus Christ of the Bible.

Salvation

Rosicrucianism does not teach that a person should trust Christ and Him *alone* for his eternal salvation. Their system is one of self-effort, their motto being, "TRY." They believe Jesus Christ never died for the sins of the world but that such teachings were added to the Bible by the Church at the Council of Nicea in 326 A.D. (see R. Swinburne Clymer, op. cit., p. 18). Clymer also states:

Man through his own individual and consciously-made efforts must attain spiritual enlightenment and ultimate immortality (Ibid, p. 19).

The Bible doctrine of salvation states that salvation is only, and completely, by grace. In fact, Paul states, "Now to the one who works, his wage is not reckoned as a favor, but as what is due. But to the one who does not work, but believes in Him who justifies the ungodly, his faith is reckoned as righteousness, just as David also speaks of the blessing upon the man to whom God reckons righteousness apart from works" (Romans 4:4-6, NASB).

Occultic Influence

Kurt Koch cites a German Rosicrucian pamphlet, *Meisterung des Lebens* which reveals its occultic teachings.

Things are made even clearer elsewhere in the booklet. The page is entitled: "The Secret World Within Us. Abilities Which We Know of and Ought to Use."
What abilities are these?

(1) "By touching letters and other objects we can become the recipients of painful messages." This is psychometry, a form of extra-sensory perception.

(2) "Thoughts or sense-impressions can be transmitted at a distance." This is an occult form of mental suggestion.

(3) "Our consciousness can suddenly see far-off places and events." This is clairvoyance by means of psychic powers.

(4) "Some people reveal their true character by magnetic radiation." This is the spiritists' idea of the so-called "aura."

In this booklet *Meisterung des Lebens*, therefore, the Order of Rosicrucians encourages its members to take up psychic and occultic practices (Kurt Koch, *Occult ABC*, Grand Rapids, MI: Int. Publs., n.d., p. 193).

Rosicrucianism does not call itself a religion but rather a secret society which "expounds a system of metaphysical and physical philosophy intended to awaken the dormant, latent faculties of the individual whereby he may utilize to a better advantage his natural talents and lead a happier and more useful life" (*Who and What Are the Rosicrucians?*, op. cit., p. 3).

However, Rosicrucianism does speak about religious matters and denies every central doctrine of the Christian faith. There are strong occult teachings in Rosicrucianism, something the Bible soundly condemns. Like Freemasonry, Rosicrucianism holds many of its practices in secret which is in contrast to Christianity, which emphasizes the open and public nature of its proclamation.

One who desires to serve Jesus Christ and His Kingdom has no business belonging to the Rosicrucian Order, working in darkness. Rather he should shout the message of Jesus Christ from the roof tops, as the Bible exhorts us:

What I tell you in the darkness, speak in the light, and what you hear whispered in your ear, proclaim upon the housetops (Matthew 10:27, NASB).

CHAPTER EIGHTEEN

Satan

K urt Koch, in his book *The Devil's Alphabet*, writes:

> The devil is a many-sided and versatile demagogue. To the psychologist he says, "I will give you new knowledge and understanding." To the occultist he will say, "I will give you the keys to the last secrets of creation." He confronts the religionist and the moralist with a mask of integrity and promises them the very help of heaven. And finally to the rationalist and the liberalist he says, "I am not there. I do not even exist."
>
> The devil is a skillful strategist. He is the master of every tactic of the battlefield. He befogs the front. He hides behind a camouflage of empty religious talk. He operates through the use of the latest scientific method. He successfully fires and launches his arguments on the social and humane plane. And his sole aim is to deceive, to entice, and to ensnare his victims (Kurt Koch, *The Devil's Alphabet*, Grand Rapids, MI: Kregel Pub., 1971, p. 7).

Satan, or the devil, has been the subject of a multitude of books and discussions for thousands of years. Some deny his existence, saying that he is merely a mythological figure. Others seem obsessed with him, seeing him behind everything imaginable.

We will explore answers to these questions: Is there such a creature? If so, what powers does he have? Who is he? Where did he come from? Should Christians fear him?

He Does Exist

The devil is real. He is not a figment of one's imagination or a mere symbol of evil; he has personal existence! He had a beginning, he is at work now, but eventually he will be judged by God. How do we know he exists?

Since it is our firm conviction that the Bible is a supernatural revelation from the true and living God, correct in everything it affirms, we can go to the Bible and see what it says about the devil and his plans.

The evangelist Billy Sunday was once asked, "Why do you believe the devil exists?" He replied, "There are two reasons. One, because the Bible says so, two, because I've done business with him."

The Career of Satan

The career of Satan begins in the distant past. God created a multitude of angels to do His bidding. In the angelic rank there was one angel who was given the highest position, guardian to the Throne of the Most High. His name was Lucifer.

Lucifer

Information about Lucifer is revealed to us in Ezekiel 28:11-19. This passage is addressed to the prince of Tyre, a man who was vain because of the wealth he possessed and thought himself to be God. While God is rebuking the prince of Tyre for his vanity, He introduces another character called the king of Tyre, the real motivator of the prince of Tyre.

> Again the word of the Lord came to me saying, "Son of man, take up a lamentation over the king of Tyre and say to him, 'Thus says the Lord God, You had the seal of perfection, full of wisdom and perfect in beauty. You were in Eden, the garden of God; every precious stone was your covering: The ruby, the topaz, and the diamond; the beryl, the onyx, and the jasper; the lapis lazuli, the turquoise, and the emerald; and the gold, the workmanship of your settings and sockets, was in you. On the day that you were created they were prepared. You were the anointed cherub who covers; and I placed you there. You were on the holy mountain of God; you walked in the midst of the stones of fire. You were blameless

in your ways from the day you were created, until unrighteousness was found in you'" (Ezekiel 28:11-15, NASB).

In his doctrinal treatise, *Satan*, Lewis Sperry Chafer comments:

According to the Scriptures, the supreme motive of Satan is his purpose to become like the Most High and, though that purpose was formed even before the age of man, it has been his constant actuating motive from that time until now. It is also the teaching of the Scriptures that Satan is in especial authority in the present age; he being permitted the exercise of his own power in order that he, and all his followers, may make their final demonstration to the whole universe of the utter folly of their claims and of their abject helplessness when wholly independent of their Creator. This is definitely predicted in 2 Timothy 3:9 as the final outcome of the attitude of the world in its independence toward God: "They shall proceed no further: for their folly shall be manifest unto all men" (Lewis Sperry Chafer, *Satan*, Philadelphia, PA: Sunday School Times Co., 1972, p. 73).

The king of Tyre is Lucifer. He was perfect in all his ways, the highest ranking celestial being, the most beautiful and wise of all God's creation.

Lucifer, along with the other angels at this time, was in perfect harmony with God. There was no rebellion. There was not any dissent; there was only one will in the universe, the will of God. Everything was beautiful and harmonious.

The Fall of Lucifer

Everything was harmonious until one day Lucifer decided to rebel against God. The prophet Isaiah reveals the unrighteousness in Lucifer:

How art thou fallen from heaven, O Lucifer, son of the morning! How art thou cut down to the ground, which didst weaken the nations! For thou hast said in thine heart, "I will ascend into heaven, I will exalt my throne above the stars of God: I will sit upon the mount of the congregation, in the sides of the north: I will ascend above the heights of the clouds: I will be like the Most High" (Isaiah 14:12-14, KJV).

Donald Grey Barnhouse states concerning the fall:

124

The next verse in Ezekiel's account gives us the key to the origin of evil in this universe. "Thou wast perfect in thy ways from the day that thou wast created, till iniquity was found in thee" (verse 15). What this iniquity was is revealed to us in some detail in the prophecy of Isaiah, but there are already interesting indications in our passage that we may not pass by. The fact given here is that iniquity came by what we might term spontaneous generation in the heart of this being in whom such magnificence of power and beauty had been combined and to whom such authority and privilege had been given. Here is the beginning of sin. Iniquity was found in the heart of Lucifer (Donald Grey Barnhouse, *The Invisible War*, Grand Rapids, MI: Zondervan Publishing House, 1965, p. 30).

He then comments on Satan's fall in the Isaiah passage:

Comparing this passage with the one in Ezekiel, it is evident that the origin of sin in the pride of Satan was soon followed by the outward manifestation of a rebellion of his will against the will of God (Ibid., p. 41).

The Emergence of Satan

The sin of Lucifer was rebellion. Five times Lucifer said in his heart, "I will."

- I will ascend into heaven;
- I will exalt my throne above the stars of God;
- I will sit upon the mount of the congregation;
- I will ascend above the heights of the clouds;
- I will be like the Most High.

This rebellion brought the downfall of Lucifer, for when Lucifer fell he was transformed into Satan. By bringing another will into the universe, a will which was antagonistic to God, the once harmonious universe was now in disharmony. When Lucifer rebelled, many of the angels rebelled with him, attempting to overthrow the authority of God. This resulted in Lucifer and his cohorts being banished from both God's presence and His favor.

It needs to be stressed at this point that God did not create the devil. We are often asked, "Why would a good God create the devil?" The answer is, "He didn't." God created Lucifer, the highest ranking of the angels, giving him beauty and intelligence and a superior position to every other created thing. He also gave Lucifer a free will to do as he pleased.

Eventually, Lucifer decided to stage a rebellion against God, and it was at this point that he became known as the devil or the adversary. He was not created for that purpose, nor did God desire for Lucifer to act independently of His will. However, Lucifer did rebel and consequently became the enemy of God and His work.

The Creation of the Universe

After the angelic revolt God created the universe as we know it today. We are not told what things were like before God created, so all we can do is speculate. The Bible says, "In the beginning God created the heavens and the earth" (Genesis 1:1). Genesis 1 reveals God's creative efforts. The last and greatest of His creation was man.

The Creation of Man

The Bible makes it clear that man was created by God in His image: "Then God said, 'Let us make man in our image, according to our likeness; and let them rule over the fish of the sea and over the birds of the sky, and over the cattle and over all the earth, and over every creeping thing that creeps on the earth.' So God created man in His own image, in the image of God He created him: male and female He created them" (Genesis 1:26, 27, NASB).

Man was God's crown of creation. He was placed in a perfect environment with everything conceivable going for him. He was in harmony with God, nature, his fellow man and himself.

The Fall of Man

However, Satan was envious of that special relationship God had with man. In Genesis 3 there is an account of what transpired when Satan appeared to Adam and Eve in the Garden of Eden in the form of a serpent.

Now the serpent was more crafty than any beast of the field which the Lord God had made. And he said to the woman, "Indeed, has God said, 'You shall not eat from any tree of the garden'?" And the woman said to the serpent, "From the fruit of the trees of the garden we may eat; but from the fruit of the tree which is in middle of the garden, God has said, 'You shall not eat from it or touch it, lest you die.' " And the serpent said to the woman, "You surely shall not die! For God knows that in the day you eat from it your eyes will be opened, and you will be like God, knowing good and evil" (Genesis 3:1-5 NASB).

The result of the yielding to temptation was a break in that special relationship between God and man.

After the Fall

Since the Garden of Eden episode, God and Satan have been locked into one great cosmic battle with man as the prize. God is attempting to bring mankind back into a right relationship with Him, while Satan is trying to pull man away from God. Moreover, the Scripture says that unbelieving man is blinded spiritually by Satan in an effort to keep him from coming to Christ.

> And even if our gospel is veiled, it is veiled to those who are perishing, in whose case the god of this world has blinded the minds of the unbelieving, that they might not see the light of the Gospel of the glory of Christ, who is the image of God (2 Corinthians 4:3, 4, NASB).

This passage is highly instructive. Satan is called the "god of this world," hiding the gospel of Christ from the minds of the unbelieving people. He will do anything to keep people from knowing God. Besides being called "the god of this world," Satan has been given other titles in Scripture which describe his character and his methods. These include:

> (1) *Devil* (John 8:44) is a Greek word meaning "the accuser and slanderer." By calling him this, one is saying that he makes a false accusation against another, one whose aim it is to harm God and man; one who will tell lies of any kind to achieve his end. The popular phrase, "The devil made me do it," (popularized by Flip Wilson) is really a cop-out. You did it because you made the choice to follow your old, sinful nature. The devil tempts!

> (2) *Satan* (Matthew 12:26) is a Hebrew word meaning "the resistor or adversary." By calling him this, one is saying that he reigns over a kingdom of darkness organized in opposition to God. In *The Bible, the Supernatural and the Jews*, McCandlish Phillips says: "Satan is a living creature. He is not corporeal. He is a spiritual being but that does not make him any less real. The fact that he is invisible and powerful greatly serves him in the pursuit

of his cause. The idea that Satan is a term for a generalized influence of evil — instead of the name of a specific living personality — is a strictly anti-biblical idea...The less you know about Satan, the better he likes it. Your ignorance of his tactics confers an advantage upon him, but he prefers that you do not even credit his existence."

(3) *Tempter* (Matthew 4:3) describes the enemy's manner of acting. Not content with denouncing before God the faults of men, he seeks to lead them into sin, because he himself is a sinner. For that reason he is called the tempter. He tempts men by promising them, as a reward for disobeying God, delights, or earthly power, or a knowledge like that of God.

(4) *Father of Lies* (John 8:44) describes one of his many tactics. To accomplish his task of tempting men by promising him things, the enemy must lie. Therefore, because he makes great use of lies, he is rightfully given this title. He is not just a liar, he is the father of lies. He hates what God loves and loves what God hates.

(5) *Lord of Death* (Hebrews 2:14). The enemy has the power of death because he can accuse sinful man. When the Son enters mankind and confronts the enemy with a human righteousness which the enemy cannot accuse, the enemy is destroyed and man is set free.

(6) *Beelzebub* (Mark 3:22, 23) ascribes to the enemy a name meaning "lord of the dunghill" or "lord of the flies." The word is generally believed to be a corruption of Baalzebub, the name of a Philistine god who was considered by the Jews to be very evil (2 Kings 1:2, 3).

(7) *Belial* (2 Corinthians 6:15) is a name which originally could be applied to any wicked person. Here it is used as a synonym of the enemy. The word itself means "worthlessness," here used as the embodiment of all "worthlessness," the enemy.

(8) *Evil One* (1 John 2:13). The total effect of all the biblical references is to present the picture of the enemy as one who is the supreme evildoer. For that reason he is given this title.

(9) *Ruler of This World* (John 14:30). Since the world, according to the Bible, is mankind in opposition to God, the enemy as the inspirer and leader of that opposition is given this title, and because his power and might are operative in the present world, he is accorded this title. Similar to this, in 2 Corinthians the enemy is even called

"the god of this world." The two titles should give us some idea of the tremendous scope of Satan's power and activity on the earth.

(10) *Prince of the Power of the Air* (Ephesians 2:1, 2). The enemy's power, in our age, is operative not only on the earth, but in space (David W. Hoover, *How to Respond to the Occult*, St. Louis, MO: Concordia Pub. House, 1977, pp. 13, 14).

In the *Dictionary of Satan* mention is made of various names given to Satan:

> *Malleus Maleficarum*, a fifteenth-century treatise by Heinrich Kramer and Jakob Sprenger, indicates that Satan may be invoked under several names, each with a special etymological significance:
> As Asmodeus, he is the Creature of Judgment. As Satan, he becomes the Adversary. As Behemoth, he is the Beast. Diabolus, the Devil, signifies two morsels: the body and the soul, both of which he kills. Demon connotes Cunning over Blood. Belial, Without a Master. Beelzebub, Lord of Flies.
> Here are the names by which he is generally known in various languages:

Arabic:	Sheitan
Biblical:	Asmodeus (or Belial or Apollyon)
Egyptian:	Set
Japanese	O Yama
Persian:	Dev
Russian:	Tchort
Syriac:	Beherit
Welsh:	Pwcca

> (Wade Baskin, *Dictionary of Satan*, NY: Philosophical Library, 1972, p. 233).

Satan's Strategy

One of Satan's plans is to convince the world that he does not exist. Denis deRougemont makes the following insightful observation:

> Satan dissembles himself behind his own image. He chooses to don a grotesque appearance which has the sure effect of making him inoffensive in the eyes of educated people. For if the devil is simply the red demon armed with a large trident, or the faun with goatee and the long tail of popular legend, who would still go to the trouble of believing in him, or even of declaring that he does not believe in him? .... What appears

to be incredible is not the devil, not the angels, but rather the candor and the credulity of the skeptics, and the unpardonable sophism of which they show themselves to be the victims: "The devil *is* a gent with red horns and a long tail: *therefore* I don't believe in the devil." And so the devil has them precisely where he wants them (Denis deRougemont, *The Devil's Share*, pp. 19-21, cited by D. G. Kehl in *Demon Possession*, ed., John Warwick Montgomery, Minneapolis, MN: Bethany Fellowship, 1976, p. 112).

In *The Screwtape Letters*, a fiction work by noted Christian thinker, C. S. Lewis, the demon is recorded instructing his apprentice as follows:

> I wonder you should ask me whether it is essential to keep the patient in ignorance of your own existence.... Our policy, for the moment, is to conceal ourselves. Of course, this has not always been so. We are really faced with a cruel dilemma. When the humans disbelieve in our existence, we lose all the pleasing results of direct terrorism, and we make no magicians. On the other hand, when they believe in us, we cannot make them materialists and skeptics.... The fact that "devils" are predominantly *comic* figures in the modern imagination will help you. If any faint suspicion of your existence begins to arise in his mind, suggest to him a picture of something in red tights, and persuade him that since he cannot believe in that...he therefore cannot believe in you (C. S. Lewis, *The Screwtape Letters*, New York: MacMillan Publ. Co., 1961, pp. 39, 40).

There are many false teachers today who encourage people to believe that they do not need to go the way of the cross. The Scriptures warn us against these individuals:

> But false prophets also arose among the people, just as there will also be false teachers among you, who will secretly introduce destructive heresies, even denying the Master who brought them, bringing swift destruction upon themselves (2 Peter 2:1, NASB).

Chafer has some apt observations concerning false prophets:

> False teachers usually are sincere and full of humanitarian zeal, but they are unregenerate. This judgment necessarily follows when it is understood that they deny the only ground of redemption. Being unregenerate, it is said of them: "But the natural man receiveth not the things of the Spirit of God: for they are foolishness unto him: neither can he know them,

because they are spiritually discerned" (1 Corinthians 2:14). Such religious leaders may be highly educated and able to speak with authority on every aspect of human knowledge, but if they are not born again, their judgment in spiritual matters is worthless and misleading. All teachers are to be judged by their attitude toward the doctrine of the blood redemption of Christ, rather than by their winsome personalities, or by their sincerity (Chafer, *Satan*, op. cit., p. 78).

Satan will use whatever method he can to keep people from coming to Christ. If a person has done many things wrong in his life and feels guilty about them, Satan will attempt to convince that person he is not good enough for God, that God would never accept him. Many people never come to God because they do not feel God could ever forgive them.

The Bible teaches that anyone may come to Christ regardless of what he has done and receive forgiveness. The Scriptures say, "Come unto me, all who are weary and heavy-laden, and I will give you rest" (Matthew 11:28, NASB). Jesus further stated, "All that the Father gives Me shall come to Me and the one who comes to Me I will certainly not cast out" (John 6:37, NASB). The Bible teaches that forgiveness is available to all those who will come to Christ no matter what they have done.

There is another type of person who is also deceived by Satan but who has the opposite problem. That person, rather than feeling he is too bad to come to God, feels that he is too good to need God. Since he has never done anything in his life which he considers horrible, he does not feel that he needs a Savior. This person is willing to go before God based upon his own merit, on the good works he has done in his life, feeling that God will certainly accept him. However, the Scriptures say, "...All have sinned and fall short of the glory of God (Romans 3:23), and "...The wages of sin is death, but the free gift of God is eternal life in Christ Jesus our Lord (Romans 6:23, NASB).

Satan's Destiny

Satan is living on borrowed time. God has promised in His Word that Satan and his angels will receive everlasting punishment for the crimes they have committed against God and man.

Then He will also say to those on His left, "Depart from Me, accursed ones, into the eternal fire which has been prepared for the devil and his angels" (Matthew 25:41, NASB).

And the devil who deceived them was thrown into the lake of fire and brimstone, where the beast and false prophet are also: and they will be tormented day and night forever and ever (Revelation 20:10, NASB).

At that time Satan will be banished once and for all from God's presence without ever again being able to inflict misery on anyone. His eternal separation from God and punishment will be a just end to his inglorious career as the prince of darkness.

C. Fred Dickason in *Angels: Elect and Evil* comments on Satan's destiny.

> The Lord Jesus, the Creator and Sovereign, will judge all creatures, including evil angels (John 5:22). He defeated Satan and his demons during His career by invading Satan's territory and casting out demons from those possessed (Matthew 12:28-29). He anticipated the final defeat of Satan when His disciples returned with reports of demons being subject to them through Christ's power (Matthew 10:1, 17-20).
>
> Through His death and resurrection, Christ sealed the final judgment of Satan and demons. The cross reveals God's hatred and judgment of all sin. The just One had to die if the unjust ones were to be forgiven (1 Peter 3:18) (C. Fred Dickason, *Angels: Elect and Evil*, Chicago, IL: Moody Press, 1975, pp. 210, 212).

What Should Be Our Attitude Toward Satan?

The Scriptures exhort us to take the proper attitude toward Satan in order to deal effectively with his onslaughts. We urge you to observe the following biblical injunctions:

(1) *Be Aware That He Exists*. The Scriptures teach that Satan exists but that he also attempts to hide that fact from the world. "And no wonder, for even Satan disguises himself as an angel of light. Therefore, it is not surprising if his servants also disguise themselves as servants of righteousness: whose end shall be according to their deeds" (2 Corinthians 11:14, 15, NASB). We have already indicated that one of Satan's schemes is to have people believe that he is a symbolic figure of evil. He would love people to see him as an "angel of light" or even as a funny

132

little man with a red suit and pitchfork rather than as the dangerous, evil, but ultimately doomed adversary of the Lord God and all mankind.

(2) *Be Aware of His Motives.* From the time of his rebellion until his ultimate destruction Satan has wanted to be like the Most High. He wants adoration. He wants allegiance. He wants the service of people who rightly should be serving God. He wants people to believe that it is he who is good and it is God who is bad. However, the worship he desires is not informed worship of a god one knows and has seriously considered.

His deception has people worshipping and serving him without even being aware of what they are doing. He wants to prepare the world for his own world rule through the antichrist immediately before the Second Coming of Jesus Christ. Lewis Sperry Chafer makes the following insightful observation:

> Even fallen humanity would not at first acknowledge Satan as its object of worship and its federal head; and such a condition of society wherein Satan will be received as supreme, as he will be in the person of the first Beast of Revelation 13, must, therefore, be developed by increasing irreverence and lawlessness toward God. Thus it has been necessary for Satan to conceal his person and projects from the very people over whom he is in authority and in whom he is the energizing power. For this reason this class of humanity believes least in his reality, and ignorantly rejects its real leader as being a mythical person. When he is worshipped, it is through some idol as a medium, or through his own impersonation of Jehovah; and when he rules, it is by what seems to be the voice of a king or the voice of the people. However, the appalling irreverence of the world today is the sure preparation for the forthcoming direct manifestation of Satan, as predicted in Daniel 9; 2 Thessalonians 2; and Revelation 13 (Lewis Sperry Chafer, *Satan*, Grand Rapids, MI: Zondervan, 1919, pp. 64, 65).

(3) *Be Aware of His Methods.* The Scriptures tell us to be aware of the devices of the devil, for his desire is to destroy the believer.

> Be of sober spirit, be on the alert. Your adversary, the devil, prowls about like a roaring lion, seeking someone to devour (1 Peter 5:8, NASB).

One of his methods is deception. From the time he deceived Eve in the Garden of Eden until the present day, Satan has been a liar. The Scriptures say:

> ...The one whose coming is in accord with the activity of Satan, with all power and signs and false wonders. And with all the deceptions of wickedness for those who perish, because they did not receive the love of the truth so as to be saved (2 Thessalonians 1:9, 10, NASB).
>
> And the great dragon was thrown down, the serpent of old who is called the devil and Satan, who deceives the whole world... (Revelation 12:9, NASB).
>
> You are of your father the devil, and you want to do the desires of your father. He was a murderer from the beginning, and does not stand in the truth, because there is no truth in him. Whenever he speaks a lie, he speaks from his own nature; for he is a liar, and the father of lies (John 8:44, NASB).

His deception comes in a variety of forms. One of his favorite schemes is to try to make a person feel content without Jesus Christ. If someone does not feel a need for God, he will not turn to God. Therefore, Satan attempts to keep people satisfied just enough that they will not turn to Christ.

In many cases the alcoholic on skid row is much closer to coming to Christ than the successful businessman who thinks he has everything he wants. We often feel that the alcoholic on skid row is exactly where Satan wants him. This is not necessarily so. The alcoholic knows he has a need, knows he has a problem and may be more likely to seek help than the successful businessman who feels content. This subtle type of deception is one of the favorite ploys of the devil.

Another deception used by Satan is counterfeiting. Whatever God has done throughout history, Satan has attempted to counterfeit it. The main counterfeit is religion. Satan loves for people to be religious, to go to church, to think things stand right between themselves and God when just the opposite is true.

If a person believes in some religion without receiving Christ as his Lord and Savior, that person is lost even though he thinks things between him and God are fine. The religious man, trusting in his own works, can be an example of deception by Satan, for God has informed us that to be in a right relationship with Him we must go the way of the cross, the death of Christ for our sins.

We must also acknowledge that apart from Christ we cannot know God. Satan wants people to believe this is not so. Christians are accused of being "narrow-minded" in saying Jesus is the only way one can get to God. The Bible tells us what God thinks of those who try to play down the need for the death of Christ on the cross:

> From that time Jesus began to show His disciples that He must go to Jerusalem and suffer many things from the elders and chief priests and scribes and be killed, and be raised up on the third day. And Peter took Him aside and began to rebuke Him saying, "God forbid it, Lord! This shall never happen to you." But He turned and said to Peter, "Get behind Me Satan! You are a stumbling block to Me; for you are not setting your mind on God's interests, but man's" (Matthew 16:21-23, NASB).

The Lord was acknowledging the sharp contrast between God's ways and fallen man's ways which are actually identified with Satan's ways. Satan cannot trust in the power of God because he has rejected God. Fallen man has also rejected God (Romans 3:12) and can turn to God only through the mediating sacrifice of Jesus Christ.

Fallen man, often with the approval and help of Satan, has developed a wide variety of religious beliefs in the world as ways to achieve God's favor without submitting to God. Satan is always pleased when people trust in their religiosity rather than Jesus Christ.

(4) *Be Aware of His Limitations.* Satan, the great deceiver, sometimes tries to fool people into thinking he is greater than he actually is. One of the misconceptions that people have about Satan is that he is like God. Nothing could be further from the truth!

God is infinite while Satan is finite or limited. God can be present everywhere at once; Satan cannot. God is all-knowing, able to read our very thoughts; Satan cannot. God is all-powerful; Satan is not. God has the ability to do anything; Satan cannot. However, Satan would like people to believe he has these abilities. Unfortunately, there are too many believers who see Satan behind

everything, giving him credit where no credit is due. Basil
Jackson makes an appropriate comment:

> Today, I believe we are seeing a most unhealthy interest in
> the area of demonology so that many of our evangelical
> friends have, in effect, become "demonophiliacs" as a result
> of their fascination with the occult. They tend to see a demon
> under every tree and, thus, quite commonly today, we hear of
> demons of tobacco, alcohol, asthma, and every other con-
> dition imaginable. In this connection, it is noteworthy that,
> by far, the majority of cases of demon possession which are
> diagnosed in the deliverance ministry today are mental in
> phenomenology. This is in marked contrast with the only
> safe records we have of accurately diagnosed cases of demon
> possession—namely, the Gospels, in which at least half the
> people possessed had physical problems rather than any
> psychiatric difficulties (Basil Jackson in *Demon Possession*,
> edited by John Warwick Montgomery, Minneapolis, MN:
> Bethany Fellowship, 1976, p. 201).

The Scriptures tell us, "You are from God, little
children, and have overcome them; because greater is He
who is in you than he who is in the world" (1 John 1:4,
NASB).

We need to realize that Satan is not all-powerful; he has
been defeated by Christ's death on the cross. The power of
sin over us is broken. Therefore, we need to respect his
power but not fear it to the point of thinking he can in-
dwell believers and make them do things they do not wish
to do. The power of God is greater but the great deceiver
would have you doubting that. Therefore, be aware of the
limitations of Satan and the unlimited power of God.

The Bible says Christ came into the world to destroy the
works of the devil (1 John 5:8). This has now been accomplished. The victory has been won. Satan has been
defeated.

The Scripture exhorts us to "put on the full armor of
God that you may be able to stand firm against the
schemes of the devil" (Ephesians 6:11, NASB). In order to
stand firm, we need to recognize that the devil exists,
what his methods and motives are, and the limitations
which he has. Knowing this we can intelligently combat
Satan and his attacks by following the principles God has
given to us:

136

Put on the full armor of God, that you may be able to stand firm against the schemes of the devil. For our struggle is not against flesh and blood, but against the rulers, against the powers, against the world forces of this darkness, against the spiritual forces of wickedness in the heavenly places. Therefore, take up the full armor of God, that you may be able to resist in the evil day, and having done everything, to stand firm. Stand firm therefore, having girded your loins with truth, and having put on the breastplate of righteousness, and having shod your feet with the preparation of the gospel of peace; in addition to all, taking up the shield of faith with which you will be able to extinguish all the flaming missiles of the evil one. And take the helmet of salvation, and the sword of the Spirit, which is the Word of God (Ephesians 6:11-17, NASB).

CHAPTER NINETEEN

Satanism

T he worship of Satan has deep historical roots. Known as
Satanism, it is found expressed in various ways. Black
magic, the Black Mass, facets of the drug culture, and
blood sacrifice all have connections with Satanism.

In *Escape from Witchcraft*, Roberta Blankenship explains what two girls, both Satanists, wrote to her as part
of their initiation ritual:

> They had had to go to a graveyard in the dead of night, walk
> across a man-sized cross, and denounce any belief in Christ.
> Afterwards, a ritual was performed and the girls had to drink
> the blood of animals that had been skinned alive (Roberta
> Blankenship, *Escape From Witchcraft*, Grand Rapids, MI:
> Zondervan Publishing House, 1972, p. 1).

Lynn Walker comments:

> In April, 1973, the battered, mutilated body of a 17-year-old
> boy, Ross "Mike" Cochran, was found outside of Daytona
> Beach, Florida. An Associated Press story said, "The verdict
> of police is that Cochran was the victim of devil worshippers:
> killed in a frenzied sacrificial ritual."
> Lynn McMillon, Oklahoma Christian College professor,
> reports, "... one variety of Satanism consists primarily of sex
> clubs that embellish their orgies with Satanist rituals.
> Another variety of Satanists are the drug-oriented groups"
> (Lynn Walker, *Supernatural Power and the Occult*, Austin,
> TX: Firm Foundation Publishing House, n.d., p. 1).

Traditional Satanism

Until contemporary times Satanism has had much more secretive associations than at present. In the past, the anti-religious and anti-god aspect was prevalent in all aspects of Satanism. Although this is not true of modern Satanism today, traditional Satanism still is associated with black magic and ritualism.

The worship of a personal and powerful devil is central to traditional Satanism. Those involved reject Christianity, yet choose the Lucifer of Scriptures as their god. The Occult Sourcebook comments:

> Traditionally, Satanism has been interpreted as the worship of evil, a religion founded upon the very principles which Christianity rejects. As such, Satanism exists only where Christianity exists, and can be understood only in the context of the Christian worldview. Things are, so to speak, reversed—the Christian devil becomes the Satanist's god, Christian virtues become vices, and vices are turned into virtues. Life is interpreted as a constant battle between the powers of light and darkness, and the Satanist fights on the side of darkness, believing that ultimately this will achieve victory (Neville Drury and Gregory Tillett, *The Occult Sourcebook*, London: Routledge & Kegan Paul, Ltd., 1978, p. 149).

Satanic witchcraft is to be found under this category of Satanism, where witches are involved in the darkest side of evil.

The recent onslaught of drugs and sexual perversion associated with the devil can be found here.

Modern Satanism

Traditional Satanism is still very prevalent, and growing in society today. However, in recent times, with the growing secularization of society and decline of Judeo-Christian morality, a new humanistic Satanism has emerged and drawn a strong following. The Church of Satan is the clearest example of this new emphasis.

> In modern times groups have emerged in England and Europe, and particularly in the United States, which, taking advantage of the permissiveness of modern society, have encouraged some publicity. The most famous of these has been the Church of Satan, founded in San Francisco in 1966 by

Anton La Vey, which currently has a membership of many thousands, and has established itself as a church throughout the United States.

Several other groups in America have imitated it, and some groups have also been established as "black witchcraft" covens. The Manson gang, in which a bizarre mixture of Satanism and occultism was practiced, gained a great deal of unfavorable publicity for Satanism in America, but in fact this resulted in a greater public interest in the subject. With more people rejecting the traditional values of morality, the Satanist movement will inevitably have greater appeal (Drury, op. cit., p. 154).

In a chapter on Satanism today, William Petersen in *Those Curious New Cults* comments on the fact that since the mid-1960s Satanism is making a comeback. He points to the catalyst for the strong upswing as being the box office smash of "Rosemary's Baby." Of the film he states:

> Anton Szandor La Vey, self-styled high priest of San Francisco's First Church of Satan and author of *The Satanic Bible*, played the role of the devil. Later, he called the film the "best paid commercial for Satanism since the Inquisition." No doubt it was (William J. Petersen, *Those Curious New Cults*, New Canaan, CT: Keats Publishing, Inc., 1973, p. 75).

Many people are becoming involved in Satanism from all walks of life. They vary in age, occupation and educational background.

Church of Satan

Although the Church of Satan sounds like a contradiction in terms, it was founded in San Francisco in 1966 by Anton Szandor La Vey. The emphasis of the Satanic church is on materialism and hedonism. Satan, to followers of this church, is more of a symbol than a reality. In this emphasis they depart from other forms of Satanism. They are interested in the carnal and worldly pleasures mankind offers.

La Vey is of Russian, Alsatian and Rumanian descent, whose past jobs have been with the circus, an organ player in nightclubs and a police photographer. All during this time La Vey was studying the occult.

Of the church La Vey declares it is:

A temple of glorious indulgence that would be fun for people.... But the main purpose was to gather a group of like-minded individuals together for the use of their combined energies in calling up the dark force in nature that is called Satan (Drury, *Occult Sourcebook, op. cit., p. 77).*

Of Satanism La Vey believes:

It is a blatantly selfish, brutal religion. It is based on the belief that man is inherently a selfish, violent creature, that life is a Darwinian struggle for survival of the fittest, that the earth will be ruled by those who fight to win (Ibid, p. 78).

Emphases of the Church

La Vey is currently the High Priest of the church, which espouses any type of sexual activity that satisfies your needs, be it heterosexuality, homosexuality, adultery or faithfulness in marriage. Part of La Vey's philosophy is expressed here:

I don't believe that magic is supernatural, only that it is supernormal. That is, it works for reasons science cannot yet understand. As a shaman or magician, I am concerned with obtaining *recipes.* As a scientist, you seek *formulas.* When I make a soup, I don't care about the chemical reactions between the potatoes and the carrots. I only care about how to get the flavor of soup I seek. In the same way, when I want to hex someone, I don't care about the scientific mechanisms involved whether they be psychosomatic, psychological, or what-not. My concern is with how to best hex someone. As a magician, my concern is with effectively *doing* the thing, not with the scientist's job of *explaining* it (La Vey 1968) (Marcello Truzzi, "Toward a Sociology of the Occult: Notes on Modern Witchcraft," *Religious Movements in Contemporary America,* ed. by Irving I. Zaretsky and Mark P. Leone, Princeton: Princeton University Press, 1974, p. 631).

Truzzi describes the church here:

Finally, we come to the major Satanic society operating in the United States today. This is the international Church of Satan. This group is legally recognized as a church, has a developed hierarchy and bureaucratic structure which defines it as no longer a cult, and claims over 10,000 members around the world. Most of these members are, in fact, merely mail-order and geographically isolated joiners, but there are clearly at least several hundred fully participating and disciplined members in the various Grottos (as their fellowships are called) set up around the world. Grottos are growing up rapidly around this country with about a dozen now in operation.

The church's High Priest and founder, Anton Szandor La Vey, whose headquarters are in San Francisco, has written *The Satanic Bible* (La Vey 1969) which has already reportedly sold over 250,000 copies and is now in its third paperback printing. La Vey also publishes a monthly newsletter for those members who subscribe to it, conducts a newspaper column in which he advises those who write in questions, and he has recently written a book on man-catching for the would-be Satanic witch (Ibid, p. 632).

There is a list of nine Satanic statements to which all members must agree. These are that Satan represents indulgence, vital existence, undefiled wisdom, kindness only to those who deserve it, vengeance, responsibility only to those who are responsible, the animal nature of man, all the "so-called sins," and "the best friend the church has ever had, as he has kept it in business all these years."

The Satanic Church is strongly materialistic as well as being anti-Christian. Pleasure-seeking could well describe their philosophy of life. What the world has to offer through the devil is taken full advantage of in the Church of Satan.

CHAPTER TWENTY

Spiritism (Necromancy)

Spiritism (sometimes called spiritualism) is the oldest form of religious conterfeit known to man. Its roots go back to the beginning of time. The Bible speaks of spiritistic practices going back as far as ancient Egypt. The Book of Exodus records the Egyptians' many occultic activities, including magic, sorcery and speaking to the dead (Exodus 7 and 8).

What is spiritism? A secular book, *The Dictionary of Mysticism*, defines spiritualism (spiritism) as "the science, philosophy and religion of continuous life, based upon the demonstrated fact of communication, by means of mediumship, with those who live in the spirit world. Spiritualism rejects the belief in physical reincarnation, but teaches that death is a new birth into a spiritual body, without any change in individuality and character, and without impairment of memory" (Frank Gaynor, ed., *Dictionary of Mysticism*, New York: Citadel Press, n.d., p. 174).

The main idea behind spiritism is that the spirits of the dead have the capacity to communicate with people here on earth through mediums, individuals who act as intermediaries between the material world and the spirit world. We do not use the term spiritualism because we do not believe such practices are actually "spiritual" or approved by God. We prefer the term "spiritism," since we believe authentic mediums contact evil spirits only posing as the spirits of the dead.

Mediums usually claim to have a spirit-guide who is their initial and primary contact in the spirit world. The spirit-guide supposedly puts the medium in contact with the spirits of the departed ones. The sessions conducted by the medium are known as seances.

Spiritism, also known as necromancy, is described by Dennis Wheatley:

> This is foretelling the future with, supposedly, the aid of the dead.
>
> The usual form it takes in these days is spiritualistic seances. A number of people gather in a room with a "sensitive," as a medium is called. The medium may be a man or a woman, but, as there are more women mediums than men, I will refer to the medium as "her."
>
> The lights in the room are dimmed, the medium goes into a trance and becomes possessed. That is to say, her spirit leaves her body, which is taken over by another.
>
> With possession the personality of the medium changes. Her voice is no longer recognizable as the one she speaks with normally. If she is a cultured woman, it may become coarse and uneducated, or vice-versa; or, quite possibly, have a foreign accent, or sound like a man's voice.
>
> Sometimes the medium is tied to her chair, with the object of convincing the audience that she is incapable of moving. Then trumpets or tambourines are seen to float about above her head in the semi-darkness. At other times she exudes from the mouth a matter that is dough-like in appearance, and is called ectoplasm.
>
> But the main object of the operation is for members of the audience either to ask the spirit, who is presumed to be possessing her, about the future, or to secure news, either directly or through the possessing spirit, of people dear to them who are dead (Dennis Wheatley, *The Devil and All His Works*, New York: American Heritage Press, 1971, pp. 71, 72).

In the book, *The Challenging Counterfeit*, the author, Raphael Gasson, a former medium, warns of the subtle, yet deep dangers of spiritualism. Gasson discusses the apparitions he called up which he believes were not spirits of the dead but demonic deception.

To Gasson, a spiritualist is:

(1) One who believes in life after death.

(2) One who believes in the possibility of contacting the spirits of the dead.

(3) One who considers it his duty to spread this "good news" to mankind.

While a spiritualist medium, Gasson believed the following:

> As a former spiritualist minister and active medium, it is possible for me to say that at the time of my participation in the movement, I actually believed that these spirits were the spirits of the departed dead and that it was my duty to preach this to all those with whom I came into contact day by day (Raphael Gasson, *The Challenging Counterfeit*, Plainfield, NJ: Logos Books, 1970, p. 36).

On the abilities of a medium:

> It is possible for the medium to give a demonstration of this gift at any seance or public meeting, in a bus, train, restaurant or park. It does not require any special lighting and can be demonstrated anywhere. No form of trance condition is necessary, only the tuning in to the spirit world by the medium, who being in a passive state of mind is open to receive messages from those who presume to be the spirits of the dead (Ibid, p. 36).

Spiritism has continued on through the ages, though sometimes waning in popularity. Over 100 years ago it experienced a rebirth which has grown and now blossomed into the modern-day spiritistic movement.

The Fox Sisters

Spiritism, in its modern form, had its beginning in the United States in 1847 through two American women, Margaret and Kate Fox. When John D. Fox and his family moved into a house in Hydeville, New York, the two youngest children, Margaret and Kate, began to hear knockings in various parts of the house.

At first it was thought this was coming from mice, but when other strange phenomena were reported, like furniture moving around by itself, natural explanations seemed inadequate. Young Kate tried to contact the "spirit" which was causing all the commotion. When she would snap her fingers, there would be a mysterious knock in response.

Kate and Margaret devised a way to communicate with the alleged spirit which would reply to their questions by coded rappings. The spirit said he was Charles Rosma, who supposedly had been murdered by a former tenant of the Fox home. When portions of a human skeleton were actually found in the cellar, worldwide attention was given to the Fox sisters. Many groups, including scientists, who investigated the Fox sisters and the rappings went away baffled. Among those who investigated was the famous New York editor, Horace Greeley ("Go West, Young Man, Go West"). Greeley concluded that "whatever may be the origin or cause of the rappings, the ladies in whose presence they occur do not make them."

In 1886 the Fox sisters confessed that they were frauds. The raps were produced by cracking their toe joints. Margaret conducted a series of demonstrations showing how she did it. At the New York Academy of Music, Margaret Fox stood on a small pine table on the stage in her stocking feet and produced loud distinct raps that could be heard throughout the building.

Although later both Fox sisters repudiated their confessions, the natural source of the "spirit" manifestations had already been exposed. This did not stop the cause of spiritism, as Joseph Dunninger comments:

> Kate died in 1892, and Margaret in 1893, both dipsomaniacs. In spite of manifest fraud, the general contention of the spiritualists remains that they were the fountainhead of American Spiritualism, and believers have completely discounted the confessions. It is such simple-mindedness which discourages skeptics from free investigation (Harry Houdini and Joseph Dunninger, *Magic and Mystery*, New York: Weathervane Books, 1967, p. 189).

Other prominent spiritists after this period included Sir Arthur Conan Doyle (creator of Sherlock Holmes); philosopher and psychic, William James; and the "father" of British Spiritism, Sir Oliver Lodge.

Bishop Pike

Spiritism came to the forefront in the 1960s when Episcopal Bishop James Pike attempted to contact the spirit of his dead son. Pike's son had committed suicide and the Bishop consulted several mediums in an attempt to contact him.

While on television in Toronto, Canada, Pike met with famous medium, Arthur Ford, who through his spirit-guide gave the Bishop the following message from his son: "He wants you to definitely understand that neither you nor any other member of the family has any right to feel any sense of guilt or have any feelings that you failed him in any way" (James A. Pike with Diane Kennedy, *The Other Side: An Account of My Experiences With Psychic Phenomena*, New York: Doubleday, 1968, pp. 246, 247).

Pike, according to his own words, had "jettisoned the Trinity, the Virgin Birth and the Incarnation" and had become a believer in the world of departed spirits without any objective criteria by which to test the spirits. The Bishop died two years later after disappearing in the Judean Desert. The mediums in whom Pike had come to trust were giving his wife false comfort between the time he was lost and found dead, saying he was alive but sick in a cave. The Bishop's case became famous and led many into dabbling with spiritism.

The Seance

What happens at a seance? What is it that makes people believe that they are contacting the spirit world? William J. Petersen comments:

> Spiritualists say there are six types of seances: passivity, vocal reality, trumpet revelation, lights, transfiguration, and levitation. In one sitting, several of these might be witnessed. One former medium, Victor Ernest, describes it like this: "Seances are noted for quietness. As the participants enter and meditate, they block out their tensions, worries, anxieties and problems.... Lights are turned down at every seance. Shades are drawn in the daytime and at night."
>
> Seances always begin on time. If you come late, the spirits might be offended.
>
> After a time of meditation, an object may move. Sometimes it is a glass on the table. Sometimes it is a small board on which a message is automatically written. Then the medium may go into a trance. His body may seem to be possessed by the spirit. When he opens his mouth, the voice you hear is different from the medium's voice. In fact, the entire personality of the medium seems to have changed (William J. Petersen, *Those Curious New Cults*, New Canaan, CN: Keats Publishing Co., 1973, 1975, p. 63).

During the seance a variety of different phenomena usually occurs, including materialization, speaking through a trumpet, spirit writing, apports and the appearance of ectoplasm.

Materialization

Materialization is the term used for the appearance during the seance of the spirits of the departed in some material form. The obvious question arises, "Are these materializations real?"

The magician, Joseph Dunninger, believed all spiritistic phenomena were a result of trickery. He, like Houdini, boasted that he could explain how all so-called phenomena actually happened. One particular medium who had baffled many experts with her materializations was exposed by Dunninger. He explained it in this manner:

There wasn't anything in the room that seemed suspicious. The furniture was ordinary, and a quick glance was sufficient to show that there were no panels in the wall, nor were there any trap doors in evidence. How was it brought about? Was this lady supernatural? Were these apparent visions of faces truly genuine? Where did the voices come from?...All of these things were simple to answer. Checking up the medium's history, a day or so previous, I found that she had, some twelve years back, been married to a circus ventriloquist. This gentleman was one of the supposed believers, and mingled with the rest of the guests. He not only produced the voices, but the spirits as well. These heads were painted upon the back of his vest, and in the dark, it was only necessary for him to remove his coat, and walk about the room. Although his footsteps could not be heard upon the heavy carpet, I made sure of my analysis, by placing my ear to the floor. The pitch black room made this possible. I heard footsteps clearly. As he walked about, these spirit faces could be seen by some, but were invisible to others. They apparently vanished and reappeared, as his body assumed various positions. Upon replacing his coat, and resuming his chair, all evidence of the ghostly visions disappeared.

Madam Biederman posed as a widow. Several houses of more fashionable type, located in the more populated residential district, belonged to her. There, in all probability, she and her husband shared the harvest. It was disappointing to my newspaper friends to be enlightened, as to the *modus operandi*, which this ghost woman employed. They were quite silent after my explanation had been rendered, which was convincing, and assured me that my findings had been accepted (Houdini and Dunninger, *Magic and Mystery*, op. cit., p. 162).

Walter B. Gibson observes that materializations are infrequently used today by mediums:

> The most spectacular spirit seances are those in which materializations are produced; for if it were genuine, a materialization would be the most convincing form of psychic phenomena possible. Seances of this type have a long tradition, dating back many years. But from the standpoint of the fraudulent medium, while a materialization may be desirable, it is extremely dangerous. Many mediums who have defied detection with trick methods have come to grief when they entered the field of materialization. Supposed spirits have been seized during many a seance and turned out to be living human beings. Police have raided the lairs of false mediums and brought back trick apparatus used in the seances. Most fake mediums now eliminate physical phenomena altogether, and materialization in particular (Gibson, Walter B., *Secrets of Magic*, New York: Grosset and Dunlap, 1967, p. 140).

Trumpet Speaking

A favorite device used in seances is the trumpet through which the spirit supposedly speaks. Although it sounds impressive, it is actually a clever trick. M. Lamar Keene, a former medium who exposed many of the secrets of his trade, reveals how he performed the trumpet phenomenon:

> My real contribution to the science and art of mediumship was in creating an original trumpet phenomenon. The standard trumpet sitting takes place in the familiar darkness — sometimes with the red light, sometimes without — and voices heard speaking through the tin megaphone are said to be those of the spirits.
>
> Some mediums just sit or stand in the darkness and talk through the trumpet, but these show little initiative or imagination. Our trumpets had a luminous band so that the sitters could see them whirling around the room, hovering in space, or sometimes swinging back and forth in rhythm with a hymn.
>
> The trick was the old black art business. My partner and I,

and other confederates if we needed them, wore head-to-toe black outfits which rendered us invisible in the darkness. We could handle the trumpet with impunity even in a good red light and with the luminescent bands giving off a considerable glow.

The trumpets, as I've mentioned earlier, were made in sections and were extendable to a total length of about four feet. Thus they could be swung around with considerable speed. The sitter, thinking the trumpet was only a foot long and seeing it whizzing around close to the ceiling, assumed that it had gotten up there by defying gravity.

Some skeptics, of course, suspected wires or threads, but my special trumpet effect really bamboozled them. It bamboozled everybody and may be justly described as one of the few truly original phenomena in mediumship.

The sitter's experience was of holding the trumpet in his or her hands and feeling it vibrate with voice sounds. Yet there were no wires, no cords—nothing (M. Lamar Keene, *The Psychic Mafia*, New York: St. Martin's Press, 1976, pp. 104, 105).

Spirit Writing

A popular manifestation during many seances is the appearance of writing on blank cards known as spirit writing. The writings are supposedly messages from departed spirits. Spirit writing is another trick of the mediums. M. Lamar Keene reveals:

Among my followers a favorite phenomenon was spirit card writing. Blank cards were given to each sitter, and he or she was asked to sign his or her name. The cards were then collected and placed on a table in the center of the room, and the lights were lowered. A hymn was sung, the lights were turned on, and *voila!* the cards now bore spirit messages, signatures of dead loved ones, Bible verses, poems, personal reminiscences, and other heartwarming evidences of life after death.

There were two ways of doing this. The cards signed by the sitters could be removed from the room in the dark by confederates and the messages added, then returned before the lights were turned on. The other way was to have cards prepared in advance, including look-alike forgeries of the sitters' signatures, and simply switch these for the blank cards (Ibid, p. 109, 110).

Apports

An apport is the sudden appearance of solid objects into or through other solid objects. M. Lamar Keene, explains apports:

> I was also a whiz at apports. These were gifts from the spirits: sometimes they were worthless trinkets like rings or brooches; other times, more impressively, they were (as I've already described) objects we had stolen from the sitter.
>
> The apports, as previously described, sometimes arrived in full light and other times tumbled out of the trumpet in the dark. In exotic variations I arranged for apports to turn up in a newly baked cake, in a sandwich, or inside a shoe.
>
> Once at a church function I told a woman the spirits had apported something for her into a chocolate cake, and when she cut into it and found her necklace, she screamed, "Oh my God, this was at home in my drawer when I left to come to church!"
>
> The truth was that we had pilfered it from her purse more than a month before and she evidently hadn't missed it (Ibid, p. 110).

Table Tilting

The Dictionary of Mysticism defines table tilting as:

> The simplest form of communicating with the spirits of the dead, using a table as the instrument of communication; the medium or all those present at the seance place their hands or fingertips on the table, which eventually begins to move on by pointing a leg at letters on a board on the floor, or by rapping according to a code, spells out the messages (Gaynor, *Dictionary*, op. cit., p. 177).

Harry Houdini, the great escape artist, who was also a psychic investigator, had this to say concerning table tilting:

> The echoes by which fake mediums do their tricks would fill a volume.... Of course, so long as edicts insist on working in darkness or semi-obscurity, adequate investigations will be almost impossible. In the dimness, it is easy for the spirit-invoked to lift a table by means of a piece of steel projecting from his sleeve, or with a steel hook hidden in his vest (Houdini and Dunninger, *Magic and Mystery*, op. cit., pp. 30, 31).

Walter Gibson reveals other methods employed to lift or tilt tables:

There are cases where fraudulent mediums have caused a table to float all around the room while people walk with it, pressing their hands against the top of the table. Here, the medium requires a confederate at the opposite side of the table. Each has a special tube strapped to the underside of one wrist and concealed by the sleeve. A rod comes out of this tube and extends under the table while the hand is on top. When the hands are raised, up comes the table, but it must, of course, be lifted at both sides.

Another device is worn on the belt. It is a sort of hook that swings out and engages the table beneath the top. As the sitters rise from their chairs, two of them, situated at opposite sides, have attached their belt hooks. The table rises when they get up and stays there until released (Walter B. Gibson, *Secrets*, op. cit., pp. 131, 132).

There are others, such as Kurt Koch, who do not necessarily see all table lifting as trickery. "Occult literature is full of examples of table lifting. This form of spiritistic practice has found many severe critics and many convinced champions. Among the documents of critical rejection are the researches of the medical doctor, Gullat Mellenburg, who with a flash photograph has shown how the medium Kathleen Colicher lifts a little table by means of a rod held between her knees. One of the best proofs of authenticity is provided by the sessions of the physicist, Prof. Zollnek, with the American spiritist, Dr. Slade. Slade's levitations and apport phenomena aroused great amazement and could not, in spite of the most stringent checks and controls, be unmasked as a swindle or explained rationally" (Kurt Koch, *Christian Counseling and Occultism*, Grand Rapids, MI: Kregel Pub., 1972, pp. 41, 42).

Although it is not clear whether all table lifting phenomena can be explained through trickery, as Houdini believed, it is clear that the Bible has harsh words to say for anyone who would attempt to communicate with the dead:

As for the person who turns to mediums and to spiritists, to play the harlot after them, I will also set My face against that person and will cut him off from among his people (Leviticus 20:6, NASB).

Spirit Raps

It has already been mentioned that modern spiritism got its start when the Fox sisters created spirit rapping by secretly snapping their toe joints. Consequently, other mediums have felt it necessary to produce the same manifestation. There have been a variety of different methods employed to produce this desired effect, with the raps usually coming from the table where the medium is seated.

Walter B. Gibson reveals some of the way these mysterious raps are produced:

> With some tables, raps may be made by rubbing the side of a shoe against the table leg, the sound carrying up into the top of the table. There are old, creaky tables that are especially suited to imitation spirit raps because of their loose joints. The medium can produce raps in a slightly darkened room by careful pressure on the table top, causing noise like snaps to come from the table.
>
> Sound seems to magnify in the dark, especially while everyone listens intently, as at a seance. Hence a room that is dimly lighted always helps fake raps. Noticeable raps may be produced by setting the finger tips firmly against the top of a table. The left thumb presses against the table, and the right thumbnail is pushed against the left thumbnail. This produces an audible click, and there are fraudulent mediums who have caused a succession of mysterious raps in this simple manner, without detection.
>
> Mechanical table rappers make the best sounds.... The top of a center-legged table is hollowed out to receive an electric coil. Two wires run through the table leg and terminate in projecting points which come out of the bottom of one of the small legs. Concealed beneath the carpet, at different places in the room, are metal floor plates. Wires run from these to an adjoining room, where they are controlled by a push button. The medium takes care to place the table at one of the selected spots, and when the tiny projecting points penetrate through the carpet, a connection is formed. A confederate pushes the electric button just as he would operate a door bell, and in this manner he causes raps to come from the top of the table (Gibson, *Secrets*, op. cit., pp. 133, 134).

Spirit Photography

Most forms of psychic phenomena, although spectacular in nature, leave no lasting evidence. This is not true, however, in the case of spirit photography which supposedly offers material proof that the spirits of the dead appeared in the seance.

A spirit photograph is an ordinary photograph taken during the seance, and when developed, it reveals the faces of the dead surrounding the sitter. This photograph is offered as proof the spirits were present. However, this is another clever mediumistic trick. Walter B. Gibson reveals how this deception is accomplished:

> Back in the days of the Civil War, a photographer discovered that if an old plate was improperly cleaned, and used again, a faint trace of the original picture would remain. That was the method used in the early stages of the game, but in later years spirit photographers have allowed their subjects to bring their own plates and to watch them being developed. Still the spirit forms appear, and people pay large sums for such photographs.
>
> One neat method of producing a spirit "extra" on a visitor's own plate is by the use of a special table with a concealed electric lamp, and a developing tray with a shallow double bottom that holds a plate with small portraits already on it.
>
> The photographer takes the sitter's picture of the unprepared plate, which can be marked for later identification. He then puts the plate in the developing tray and covers it so that no light can enter. But light does get in from below, for the medium presses a hidden release and the center of the tabletop drops in two sections like a miniature trap door. The light goes on automatically, but cannot be seen because of the covered tray.
>
> The light causes the ghost portraits to be projected from the hidden plate in the double bottom of the tray to the sitter's original plate above. The medium presses the switch again, the light goes off, the trap closes, and the sitter's plate is removed from the tray. On the developed plate the sitter's portrait appears with faces hovering above, dim but recognizable, like spirits (Ibid, p. 146).

Ectoplasm

The Dictionary of Mysticism defines ectoplasm:

> Ectoplasm: A term coined by Professor Richet (a contraction of the Greek words *ektos*, exteriorized, and *plasma*, substance) for the mysterious protoplasmic substance which streams forth from the bodies of mediums, producing super-

physical phenomena, including materializations, under manipulation by a discarnate intelligence. Ectoplasm is described as matter which is invisible and impalpable in its primary state, but assuming the state of a vapor, liquid or solid, according to its stage of condensation. It emits an ozone-like smell. The ectoplasm is considered by spiritualists to be the materialization of the astral body (Gaynor, *Dictionary*, op. cit., p. 53).

However, the production of ectoplasm can be easily manufactured by the medium. The ex-medium, M. Lamar Keene, explains how he created the ectoplasm effect:

It's amazing what effects can be created in the dark, manipulating yards and yards of chiffon and gauze which appears to shimmer in the unearthly glow of the ruby light. What I did was what magicians call "black art." The parts of me not covered by ectoplasm were garbed totally in black and were quite invisible in the dark. (For trumpet sittings, which I'll explain next, I wore a head-to-toe black outfit, including a mask over my face which rendered me as unseen as The Shadow used to be in his famous adventures.)

Standing in the seance room in my invisible outfit, I would deftly unroll a ball of chiffon out to the middle of the floor and manipulate it until eventually it enveloped me. What the sitters saw was a phenomenon: A tiny ball of ectoplasm sending out shimmering tendrils which gradually grew or developed into a fully materialized spirit. Unless you have witnessed the effect under seance conditions, you'll find it hard to grasp how eerily convincing it can be.

The ectoplasmic figure could disappear the same way it appeared. I simply unwound the chiffon from my body slowly and dramatically then wadded it back into the original tiny ball. What the sitter saw was the fully formed spirit gradually disintegrate, evaporate into a puff of ectoplasm.

The variations were endless...(Keene, *Psychic Mafia*, op. cit., p. 101).

In *The Dead Do Not Talk*, Julien J. Proskauer gives an historical background of the use of ectoplasm:

Whenever gullible scientists who attend a seance witness something that they can't explain, they invent a name for it, along with a theory regarding the thing itself. In so doing, they create new targets at which mediums can aim and score a bull's-eye.

For there is nothing that a smart medium likes better than

a challenge, provided he is allowed full leeway. And a challenge based on a delusion is the best of all. The medium discovers what it was that the scientist misinterpreted and cooks up an improved method of repeating the effect. The result is always more than satisfactory.

Ectoplasm was one of those scientific "finds" that really boomed the psychic business. In simple terms, ectoplasm is "ghost stuff" and it came into existence immediately after a scientific investigator reported that he saw a parcel of it emanating from a medium.

Now the curious fact is this: If spirits chose to herald themselves in ectoplasmic style, why didn't they furnish a few samples back in the Fox cottage where the first modern manifestations began? Why didn't they float a few clouds of ectoplasm out through the windows of the cabinet in which the Davenport boys were stalling their tests because somebody had tied them with the wrong kind of knot? Why couldn't the Davenport brothers, up in the town of Chittenden, produce their Indian controls under cover of some ectoplasmic smoke, instead of waiting for evenings when the scene was tempered by an abundance of standard Vermont mist?

The best answer is to consult Podmore's *Modern Spiritualism* which still rates as one of the finest samples of debunking ever written. It appeared more than fifty years after the spook business came into vogue and covers everything with a remarkable clarity and a thorough index. Yet in that index the word "ectoplasm" does not appear.

Think of it! The masters of the other plane required a half century which included such mediums as the famous Home, before they thought of releasing the great wherewithal which no Grade-A medium of today could do without (Julien J. Proskauer, *The Dead Do Not Talk*, NY: Harper & Brothers Publishers, 1946, pp. 90, 91).

Proskauer in his chapter, "Ectoplasm is Bunk," gives some excellent illustrations and examples of the fraud involved in ectoplasm (Ibid, pp. 90-98).

Automatic Writing

Automatic writing consists of producing written material by a medium who is not in control of his conscious self. The subject matter is said to be beyond any training, experience or knowledge of the medium. Mediums also claim to be able to produce automatic drawings and automatic paintings while in their trance-like state.

How can this be accomplished? Some see the answer as a matter of "disassociation," which the clever medium uses to his advantage.

According to Louis E. Bisch, the psychologist, automatic writing is largely a matter of disassociation. One need not resort to the fanciful hypothesis that a spirit is guiding the hand of the writer, says he, in discussing the writings which mediums have promulgated while apparently in a trance. Just as one can drive an automobile and think of other things, or do some familiar work and think of last night's good time, or play a familiar piece on the piano while one's mind is miles away, so is it possible to practice disassociation in writing. Of course, some can disassociate more rapidly than others — that is a matter of natural tendency.

Disassociation is common to many normals but automatic writing is liable to be displayed by people who are prone to hysteria, in which such proclivities are heightened. Give such a person a pencil, then talk to him. Such a person will answer the questions, write about something else and talk about a distinctly different matter. The curious part of it is that the subject will be afterward entirely ignorant of what he has written. With one part of his conscious mind he was talking, with the other he wrote. The medium is canny enough to take advantage of such facts of psychology and make use of them often to the detriment of the client (Houdini and Dunninger, *Magic and Mystery*, op. cit., pp. 189, 190).

Kurt Koch feels some automatic writing is a spiritist phenomenon with occult forces at work.

In spiritist automatic writing, the medium must achieve complete inner quietness and must not concentrate on anything. Suddenly, the compulsion to write comes over the medium. One of the most versatile and powerful mediums of our day is Matthew Manning, whom we have already mentioned in another connection. A number of parapsychologists have studied Manning. Here is an example that illustrates automatic writing.

A parapsychologist visited Manning to check out some of his experiments. Manning offered to give the parapsychologist a diagnosis of his state of health. Manning took a sheet of paper and wrote the parapsychologist's date of birth at the top of the page. Then Manning waited. After a minute, his hand began to write in a quite different style of handwriting. The writing was signed at the bottom, Thomas Penn. The diagnosis that this Thomas Penn from the other side gave was also interesting. It was, "A malfunction in the epigastric region."

The parapsychologist asked Manning, "Do you know what is meant by 'the epigastric region'?" "No," said Manning, "I don't know." "It isn't altogether clear to me either," said the parapsychologist. When checked by a doctor, the diagnosis proved to be correct. This knowledge cannot therefore have come from Manning's subconscious. This is a case where extrahuman forces are at work.

Automatic drawing is on the same level. Manning takes a crayon in his hand, waits, ands then suddenly starts to draw quickly. After a few minutes his style changes. He draws in the style of well-known artists. When the parapsychologist was there, Manning drew a reproduction of the rhinoceros which Albrecht Durer drew in 1515, and which is hanging in the British Museum in London. A few minutes later, Manning drew a picture of Salome with the head of John the Baptist on a table before her. The original is by Aubrey Beardsley. I have seen both drawings and know that Manning has certainly not the artistic ability to copy the drawing of Albrecht Durer or the painting of Beardsley from memory.

Manning originally believed that his subconscious mind was responsible for all these powers. He has long since given up that view. He now believes that he receives his impulses and abilities from the unseen world (Kurt Koch, *Occult ABC*, Grand Rapids, MI: Int. Publs., n.d., pp. 220, 221).

Is It All Deception?

Harry Houdini and Joseph Dunninger exposed in their day the fraudulent practices of mediums. More recently M. Lamar Keene, the famous medium, revealed how he deceived untold thousands with his gimmicks. These individuals, along with others who are well qualified in spiritistic phenomena, believe all such practice is deception.

They strongly assert that spirits of the dead do not talk to the one sitting at the seance but rather that the medium is perpetrating a con game. Although we believe the great majority of things which happen during a seance can be rationally explained as deception, we also believe that supernatural manifestation sometimes occurs.

John Warwick Montgomery makes an appropriate comment:

Almost everyone has heard of the clever techniques of fraudulent mediums—such as inflatable rubber gloves that leave the impression of spirit hands in paraffin and then, deflated, are able to be drawn out of the hardened wax through a small hole, leaving nothing but ghostly imprints. Houdini claimed that he could duplicate by natural means any spiritistic phenomenon shown to him. And recent visitors to Disneyland have invariably been impressed by the computerized effectiveness of the "spirits" in the Haunted Mansion. Are not all occult phenomena capable of similar explanation?

Doubtless the world would be a more comfortable and secure place if the answer were yes; unfortunately, however, such an answer is not possible. Innumerable instances of occult phenomena resist categorization as "humbug" or natural occurrences in disguise (John Warwick Montgomery, *Principalities and Powers*, Minneapolis, MN: Bethany Fellowship, Inc., 1973, p. 30).

Kurt Koch responds in a similar manner:

My knowledge of spiritism is not derived from books. Counseling is the only starting point for my experience....I have been dealing with these problems in counseling for forty-five years. There are fake manifestations by spiritist mediums....I am not concerned with fake spiritism. I am only interested in describing genuine phenomena (Kurt Koch, *Occult ABC*, op. cit., p. 216).

Dr. Nandor Fodor, a man who spent a lifetime as a psychic investigator, attempted to present a legal case of survival after death with the following examples:

The protagonists of survival were ready to step before the bar. Could I, as a Doctor of Laws, put forward legally acceptable evidence?

I accepted the challenge without searching far and wide for the best reported case. There were many. I did not try to evaluate them comparatively. My space was restricted. So I picked the Pearl Tie-Pin case reported by Sir William S. Barrett in his book, *On the Threshold of the Unseen*, as the one. Barrett accepted it as remarkably evidential. Sir Oliver Lodge concurred with him.

The message about the pearl tie-pin came through Mrs. Hester Dowden, one of the best automatic writing mediums of the time. She was the daughter of the late Professor Edward Dowden, a classical scholar of Dublin. She was a lady of culture and refinement, of a singularly critical mind. I knew her personally. Her sincerity and personal integrity have never been questioned.

The message was given to Miss Geraldine Cummins, the daughter of Professor Ashley Cummins, of Cork, Ireland. Afterward, Miss Cummins herself became a remarkable automatist. This is the story as told by Sir William S. Barrett:

"Miss Cummins had a cousin, an officer with our army in France, who was killed in battle a month previously to the sitting; this she knew. One day, after the name of her cousin had unexpectedly been spelt out by the Ouija board, and her name given in answer to her query, do you know who I am? the following message came:

" 'Tell mother to give my pearl tie-pin to the girl I was going to marry. I think she ought to have it.' When asked what was the name and address of the lady, both were given; the name spelt out included the full Christian and surname, the latter being a very unusual one and quite unknown to both sitters. The address given in London was either fictitious or taken down incorrectly, as a letter sent there was returned, and the whole message was thought to be fictitious.

"Six months later, however, it was discovered that the officer had been engaged, shortly before he left for the front, to the very lady whose name was given; he had, however, told no one. Neither his cousin, nor any of his own family in Ireland were aware of the fact and had never seen the lady nor heard her name until the War Office sent over the deceased officer's effects. Then they found that he had put this lady's name in his will as his next of kin, both Christian and surname being precisely the same as given through the automatist; and what is equally remarkable, a pearl tie-pin was found in his effects.

"Both the ladies have signed a document they sent me, affirming the accuracy of the above statement. The message was recorded at the time, and not written from memory after verification had been obtained."

This, indeed, is a legal case. Because of the bequest of the pearl tie-pin, it could well have been taken into court. What would have happened if the bequest had been contested? The survival of the deceased officer was as well proven as could be demanded by legal standards but to bring a verdict stating this would have been far too embarrassing to any judge, and I have no doubt that he would have used every means of persuasion at his disposal to settle the case out of court (Dr. Nandor Fodor, *The Unaccountable*, New York: Award Books, 1968, pp. 162-164).

Stan Baldwin gives the following example:

A certain medium, Mrs. Blanche Cooler, supposedly communicated with the spirit of a man killed in battle; his name was Gordon Davies. The spirit, purporting to be Davies and speaking in a voice that sounded like his, described some unusual features of a house, foretold the future, and gave accurate information that was unknown to any of the participants in the seance and therefore was not a result of thought transference from them. This time, however, events proved the communication was not from the departed Davies, because he had not departed. He turned up alive and was shown to have had nothing whatever to do with the seance! What explanation can there be for such things? The Bible teaches that there is a company of fallen spirits which, to use an especially appropriate term, bedevil men. One such spirit enabled the girl described in Acts 16 to foretell the future. Obviously, she was not a fraud, for after the spirit left her, she could no longer bring her masters gain by telling fortunes — a result that would not have come about if she were only faking from the start (Stan Baldwin, *Games Satan Plays*, Wheaton, IL: Victor Books, cited by Clifford Wilson and John Weldon, *Occult Shock and Psychic Forces*, San Diego: Master Books, 1980, p. 99).

There is also the possibility that the medium did some investigation in the life of Mr. Davies to come up with this astounding information which is, by the way, a standard practice of many fraudulent mediums. Whether the manifestation was fraudulent or was the manifestation of an evil spirit, we at least know it was not the departed spirit of Mr. Davies.

Spiritism is not confined to the spiritualistic churches, for many of the cults engage in spiritistic activities. The Mormon Church, for example, has had occultic tendencies from the beginning as the following testimony of an ex-Mormon graphically reveals:

I began doing genealogical research even before I was baptized. From the very beginning, it was obvious that I had "help" from somewhere. Books would literally call to me from the shelves, and upon opening them I would find evidence of family lines for which Mormon Temple work needed to be done. I began teaching genealogy classes my first year as a Mormon, and was soon recognized as an expert.

Once I felt the presence of a dead grandmother with me in the temple, who I had not been able to believe would accept Mormonism even in the spirit world. Yet her presence was so real that I challenged her to help me locate her mother's records, which I had been unable to find. Two hours later in the genealogical library they "turned up" miraculously.

I knew others to whom dead relatives visibly appeared and spoke, telling of their conversion to Mormonism in the spirit world. One friend would see missing names written on her bedspread each night as she said her prayers. A voice once gave me a name that led me to records correcting false information I had accepted concerning an ancestor.

I submitted over 200 names of ancestors and performed most of the female Temple ordinances myself. Spiritist visitations and what would otherwise have been considered occultic manifestations were accepted in the name of the Church.

These supernatural experiences always came just when my testimony of the Church and Joseph Smith was wavering. For ten years I overlooked much that I knew was false and contradictory...convinced that if the spirits of dead ancestors were so anxious to have their genealogical work done, then the Mormon Church must be all that Joseph Smith had claimed.

In appearances to many Mormons, the spirits testify that the Mormon Church is the only true church, that they have accepted the "restored" gospel of Mormonism in the spirit world, and urge the living to pursue genealogical work (Dave Hunt, *The Cult Explosion*, Irvine, CA: Harvest House Publishers, 1980, p. 147).

Can the Dead Communicate With the Living?

If there is any supernatural activity in the seance, it is most certainly *not* in the spirit of the departed one speaking through the medium. It is not possible according to the Scriptures to contact the spirits of the dead! Jesus made this very clear with the account of the rich man and Lazarus.

Now there was a certain rich man and he habitually dressed in purple and fine linen, gaily living in splendor every day. And a certain poor man named Lazarus was laid at his gate, covered with sores, and longing to be fed with the crumbs which were falling from the rich man's table; besides, even the dogs were coming and licking his sores. Now it came about that the poor man died and he was carried away by the angels to Abraham's bosom; and the rich man also died and was buried. And in Hades he lifted up his eyes, being in torment and saw Abraham far away, and Lazarus in his bosom. And he cried out and said, "Father Abraham, have mercy on me, and send Lazarus, that he may dip the tip of his finger in water and cool off my tongue; for I am in agony in this flame." But Abraham said, "Child, remember that during your life you received your good things, and likewise Lazarus bad things; but now he is being comforted here, and you are in agony. And besides all this, between us and you there is a great chasm fixed, in order that those who wish to come over from here to you may not be able, and that none may cross over from there to us." And he said, "Then I beg you, Father, that you send him to my father's house—for I have five brothers—that he may warn them, lest they also come to this place of torment." But Abraham said, "They have Moses and the Prophets; let them hear them." But he said to him, "No, Father Abraham, but if someone goes to them from the dead, they will repent!" But he said to him, "If they do not listen to Moses and the Prophets, neither will they be persuaded if someone rises from the dead" (Luke 16:19-31, NASB).

Two things need to be noted about this passage:

(1) There is a great gulf fixed between the abode of the righteous dead and the unrighteous dead which no one can cross. The dead, in other words, are limited in their movement.

(2) The rich man was refused permission to warn his five brothers of their impending fate if they did not repent. The passage indicates, along with the rest of Scripture, that the dead are not allowed to speak to the living on any matter. The response in this case was that the brothers needed to believe what God had said to escape their doom rather than a voice from the dead.

Jesus declared that those who harden their hearts against the very words of God through Moses and the Prophets would not listen to one returned from the dead. This is proven by those who reject the Gospel of Jesus Christ today. Jesus Christ *did* rise from the dead, and yet people still reject His Word.

Medium at Endor

A passage of Scripture often quoted in discussions of mediums is 1 Samuel 28, the story of Saul and the medium at Endor. Proponents of spiritism cite the passage to point out that the medium was able to contact Samuel's spirit.

First, it must be stated that not all Bible scholars believe it was Samuel who was called up; some believe it was a demon, and some believe that it was a trick. But the majority of evangelical scholars hold that it actually was Samuel (Joseph Bayly, *What About Horoscopes?*, Elgin IL: David C. Cook Publ. Co., 1970, p. 71). This position can be substantiated and explained by studying the context.

First, the element of surprise by the medium indicates she was just as surprised as anyone at Samuel's appearance (v. 12).

Second, the Scripture clearly indicates that Samuel appeared (v. 12). There is no indication that either fraud or demonism is present, as should be the case if those were true.

Thus, the logical conclusion must be in keeping with Scripture. The Bible teaches that men have no power to call up dead spirits, yet Samuel did appear. One concludes that it was God who chose to raise up Samuel for this one occasion for His purposes, and there was no doubt who it was. Neither the powers of darkness (the medium) nor the poor representation of the Kingdom of Light (Saul) had any doubt as to the identity of who appeared.

God always does as He chooses in this area, just as He chose to bring back Moses and Elijah on the Mount of Transfiguration before Christ was resurrected. By means of analogy, it is also true that though all men are subject to death, neither Enoch nor Elijah died. Here again, the Lord made the exception.

The Beliefs of Spiritism

Some of the official writings of spiritism claim compatability with Christianity.

How — it may be asked — should Christianity be opposed to spiritualism when the Christian religion was really born in a seance? The real beginning of Christianity, its motive power, its great impetus, came — not from the birth or death of Jesus — but from Pentecost, the greatest seance in history (R.F. Austin, *The A.B.C. of Spiritualism*, Milwaukee, WI: National Spiritualist Association of Churches, n.d., p. 23).

However, a comparison between the beliefs of spiritism and Christianity show no agreement whatsoever. The following questions and answers are taken from a booklet distributed by the National Spiritualist Association of Churches:

Is not spiritualism based upon the Bible? (Q. 11)

No. The Bible so far as it is inspired and true is based upon mediumship and therefore, both Christianity...and spiritualism rest on the same basis. Spiritualism does not depend for its credentials and proofs upon any former revelation.

Do spiritualists believe in the divinity of Jesus? (Q. 16)

Most assuredly. They believe in the divinity of all men. Every man is divine in that he is a child of God, and inherits a spiritual (divine) nature....

Does spiritualism recognize Jesus as one person of the Trinity, co-equal with the Father, and divine in a sense in which divinity is unattainable by other men? (Q. 17)

No. Spiritualism accepts him as one of many Saviour Christs, who at different times have come into the world to lighten its darkness and show by precept and example the way of life to men. It recognizes him as a world Saviour but not as "the only name" given under heaven by which men can be saved.

Does not spiritualism recognize special value and efficacy in the death of Jesus in saving men? (Q. 19)

No. Spiritualism sees in the death of Jesus an illustration of the martyr spirit, of that unselfish and heroic devotion to humanity which ever characterized the life of Jesus, but no special atoning value in his sufferings and death....

From the standpoint of spiritualism, how is the character and work of Jesus to be interpreted? (Q. 21)

Jesus was a great Mediator, or Medium, who recognized all the fundamental principles of spiritualism and practiced them....

Does spiritualism recognize rewards and punishments in the life after death? (Q. 86)

...No man escapes punishment, no man misses due reward. The idea of an atoning sacrifice for sins which will remove their natural consequences (pardon) is simply ludicrous to the inhabitants of the spirit spheres.

Do the departed, according to spiritualism, find heaven and hell as depicted by Church teaching? (Q. 88)

Not at all....They deny any vision of a great white throne, any manifestations of a personal God, any appearance of Jesus, or any lake of fire and torment for lost souls....[cited by Edmond Gruss, *Cults and the Occult*, rev. ed., Grand Rapids, MI: Baker Book House, 1974, pp. 57, 58).

The Bible and Spiritism

The Scripture speaks loud and clear in its denunciation of any type of spiritistic practice.

You shall not allow a sorceress to live (Exodus 22:18, NASB).

You shall not eat anything with the blood nor practice divination or soothsaying (Leviticus 19:26), NASB).

Do not turn to mediums or spiritists; do not seek them out to be defiled by them. I am the Lord Your God (Leviticus 19:31, NASB).

As for the person who turns to mediums and to spiritists, to play the harlot after them, I will also set My face against that person and will cut him off from among his people (Leviticus 20:6, NASB).

Now a man or a woman who is a medium or a spiritist shall surely be put to death. They shall be stoned with stones, their bloodguiltiness is upon them (Leviticus 20:27, NASB).

When you enter the land which the Lord your God gives you, you shall not learn to imitate the detestable things of those nations. There shall not be found among you anyone who makes his son or his daughter pass through the fire, one who uses divination, one who practices witchcraft, or one who interprets omens, or a sorcerer, or one who casts a spell, or a medium, or a spiritist, or one who calls up the dead. For whoever does these things is detestable to the Lord; and because of these detestable things the Lord your God will drive them out before you (Deuteronomy 18:9-12, NASB).

And when they say to you, "Consult the mediums and spiritists who whisper and mutter, Should not a people consult their God? Should they consult the dead on behalf of the living?" (Isaiah 8:19, NASB).

There are many dangers involved in spiritism. The former medium, M. Lamar Keene, mentions one of them:

One of the most alarming things about the mediumistic racket is how completely some people put their lives into the hands of ill-educated, emotionally unbalanced individuals who claim a hot line to heaven. As a medium I was routinely asked about business decisions, marital problems, whether to have an abortion, how to improve sexual performance, and similar intimate and important subjects. That people who ask such questions of a medium are risking their mental, moral and monetary health is a shocking but quite accurate description of the matter (Keene, *Psychic Mafia*, op. cit., p. 22).

Attempting to contact the spirits of the dead is not only fruitless, it also leads one down the path of death. M. Lamar Keene reveals the reason he quit his profession:

> ...If I stayed in mediumship I saw only deepening gloom. All the mediums I've known or known about have had tragic endings.
> The Fox sisters, who started it all, wound up as alcoholic derelicts. William Slade, famed for his slate-writing tricks, died insane in a Michigan sanitarium. Margery, the medium, lay on her deathbed a hopeless drunk. The celebrated Arthur Ford fought the battle of the bottle to the very end and lost. And the inimitable Mable Riffle, boss of Camp Chesterfield—well, when she died it was winter and freezing cold, and her body had to be held until a thaw for burial; the service was in the cathedral at Chesterfield. Very few attended.
> Wherever I looked it was the same: mediums at the end of a tawdry life (Ibid., pp. 147, 148).

What a contrast this is to the life that is offered by Jesus Christ. Jesus promised, "...I came that they might have life, and might have it abundantly" (John 10:10, NASB). The Christian, rather than attempting the hopeless task of talking to the dead, can talk to the living God. He does not need to resort to mediums or spiritists.

Moreover, those who have died having a relationship with God are not dead but are spiritually alive in God's presence. Jesus pointed this out:

> But regarding the resurrection of the dead, have you not read that which was spoken to God saying, I am the God of Abraham, and the God of Isaac, and the God of Jacob? He is not the God of the dead but of the living (Matthew 22:31, 32, NASB).

Jesus Christ offers real hope. Spiritists offer a false hope that leads to the path of destruction. Contrast the bitter end of mediums and spiritists with that of a man of God, the Apostle Paul, who gave this dying declaration:

> I have fought the good fight, I have finished the course, I have kept the faith; in the future there is laid up for me the crown of righteousness, which the Lord the righteous Judge, will award to me on that day; and not only to me, but also to all who have loved his appearing (2 Timothy 4:7, 8, NASB).

CHAPTER TWENTY-ONE

Superstition

T here are many phenomena attributed to the occult which are, in reality, nothing but superstition. Superstition is a belief or practice not based upon fact but upon fear or ignorance of the unknown. Superstition is not confined to a bygone time or to primitive people, for it is with us today. The following are some examples of superstition.

The Number 13

The number 13 is supposed to bring bad luck. This is an ancient superstition still believed by many today. Many builders skip from the 12th to the 14th floor in building construction, fearing the 13th floor will bring bad luck. Some feel it is unlucky for 13 people to dine together since supposedly one of them will die within the year. Friday the 13th allegedly brings bad luck and many people are cautious about the activities they plan. No one knows how this superstition started, as Daniel Cohen comments:

> We do not know how the number 13 got its bad reputation. "Unlucky 13" may have started with the Vikings or other Norsemen. They told the story of a great banquet for 12 guests—all of them gods. The evil god Loki, angry at not being invited, sneaked into the banquet. Now there were 13 guests. One of the gods at the banquet was killed and since that time—the story goes—the number 13 has been considered unlucky.

Some think the belief started with Christianity. At the Last Supper there were 13—Jesus Christ and the 12 apostles. The Last Supper was followed by Christ's crucifixion so that again the number 13 was identified with a dreadful event. It is believed that Christ was crucified on a Friday. This explains why Friday is regarded by some superstitious people as unlucky. For example, Friday is supposed to be a bad day to start a new job, to begin a voyage, to cut one's nails, or to get married (Daniel Cohen, *A Natural History of Unnatural Things*, New York: McCall Pub. Co., 1971, pp. 5, 6).

Breaking a Mirror

Another well-known superstition involves breaking a mirror which supposedly brings the individual seven years of bad luck. This belief goes back several thousand years to when people believed the image of a person, whether a painting or a reflection, was part of that person and whatever happened to the image happened to that person.

Prayer for Sneezing

Here's a superstition we all practice without being aware of it. When a person sneezes, we say "gesundheit," which is German for "good health to you" or we might say "God bless you." Why no offer of a blessing for a cough? Why only the sneeze?

This goes back thousands of years when people believed one's spirit resided inside his head and a good sneeze might send it away! Since evil spirits were known to be lurking about trying to get into the man's head, his friends would say a prayer to keep the evil spirits away.

Daniel Cohen further illustrates the ancient idea that the spirit could get away from the body:

When you sneeze, you are supposed to cover your nose with a handkerchief. This is just good sense because a sneeze can spread germs. But why are you supposed to cover your mouth when you yawn? Not to do so is considered very rude, yet yawning spreads few or no germs. This custom, too, started thousands of years ago. At that time, a man was afraid that his spirit might escape though his open mouth or that some evil spirit might enter. So he blocked his mouth with his hand. In modern times, this ancient belief has been changed. Some parents tell their children to cover their mouths when they yawn, or a fly might get in (Ibid, p. 12).

Omens

An omen is "an event or object believed to be a sign or token portending or foretelling the evil or beneficent character of a future occurrence" (*The Dictionary of Mysticism*, op. cit., p. 130).

One medieval writer listed the following as evil omens: "If a hare cross the way at our going forth, or a mouse gnaw our clothes. If they bleed three drops at nose, the salt falls towards them, a black spot appears in their nails, etc."

Other evil omens include having a black cat cross your path and walking under a ladder.

Amulets

An amulet is an object of superstition. It can be defined as "a material object on which a charm is written or over which a charm was said, worn on the person to protect the wearer against dangers, disease, to serve as a shield against demons, ghosts, evil magic, and to bring good luck and good fortune" (Frank Gaynor, ed., *Dictionary of Mysticism*, New York: Citadel Press, n.d., p. 10).

In the ancient world, along with many present-day primitive tribes, the carrying of an amulet is a common everyday occurrence. These objects (also called fetishes, talismans, charms) supposedly ward off evil spirits or bring luck to the wearer.

CHAPTER TWENTY-TWO

Witchcraft

Witchcraft is known as the "Old Religion" and is an ancient practice dating back to biblical times. Witchcraft can be defined as the performance of magic forbidden by God for non-biblical ends. The word witchcraft is related to the old English word *wiccian*, "practice of magical arts."

It was during the Middle Ages that witchcraft experienced a great revival. It was an age where everyone believed in the supernatural and superstition abounded. Roger Hart expressed the climate in the following manner:

> The people of medieval Europe shared a deep belief in the supernatural. The kingdom of darkness, with its devils and evil spirits, was as real and personal as the Kingdom of Heaven: Magic could be as powerful as prayer.
>
> The idea of supernatural spirits was universal and ordinary folk everywhere believed in demons, imps, goblins, hobgoblins, poltergeists and other spirits, and in legendary creatures such as vampires, werewolves and unicorns (Roger Hart, *Witchcraft*, New York: G. P. Putnam's Sons, 1971, p. 11).

If someone wanted to become a witch, there was an initiation process. Some of the techniques were simple and some were complicated, but there were usually two requirements. The first requirement was that the would-be witch must join of his or her own free will. The second requirement was that the prospective witch must be willing to worship the devil.

Witches are usually organized into covens.

The word "coven" dates from about 1500 and is a variation of the word convent. It means simply an assembly of people, but it came to be applied especially to the organization of the witches' society (Geoffrey Parrinder, *Witchcraft: European and African*, London: Faber and Faber, 1963, p. 39).

Halloween

The day witches celebrate above all others is October 31, which is All Hallows Eve or Halloween. It is believed that on this night Satan and his witches have their greatest power.

The origin of Halloween goes back 2,000 years before the days of Christianity to a practice of the ancient Druids in Britain, France, Germany and the Celtic countries. The celebration honored their god Samhain, lord of the dead. The Celtic people considered November 1st as being the day of death. This was because it was the end of autumn and the beginning of winter for them.

The time of falling leaves seemed an appropriate time to celebrate death, which is exactly what Halloween was to them: A celebration of death honoring the god of the dead. The Druids believed that on this particular evening the spirits of the dead returned to their former home to visit the living.

If the living did not provide food for these evil spirits, all types of terrible things would happen to the living. If the evil spirits did not get a treat, then they would trick the living. This ancient practice is still celebrated today where people dress up as the dead, knocking on doors and saying, "Trick or treat," not realizing the origin of that which they are practicing. Nevertheless, it is still considered by witches as the night on which they have their greatest power.

Before the introduction of Christianity to these lands, the celebration of death was not called Halloween. Halloween is a form of the designation "All Hallows Eve," a holy evening instituted by the Church to honor all the saints of Church history.

Some Church historians allow the possibility that All Saints' Eve was designated October 30 to counteract the pagan influences of the celebration of death. While All

Hallows Eve began as a strictly Christian holiday, the pagan influences from earlier traditions gradually crept in while the Church's influences waned.

Today Halloween is largely a secular holiday, an excuse to get dressed up as somebody else and have a party. However, true witches and followers of witchcraft still preserve the early pagan beliefs and consider Halloween a sacred and deadly powerful time. Having turned their backs on the God of the Bible, they invoke the help of Satan, fallen from God's favor and relegated to darkness.

Witch Hunting

One of the darkest periods in European and American history was the time of the "Great Witch Hunt." Although there had been scattered instances of persecution of witches as early as the 12th century, it did not truly get started until the end of the 15th century when two significant events occurred.

The first was a papal letter (known as a Bull) issued on December 5, 1484, by Pope Innocent VIII, which instituted the beginning of official action against suspected witches. This Bull received wide circulation and in it power was granted to men who were responsible for punishing witches. These men were known as inquisitors. The Papal Bull contained the following:

> Desiring with the most profound anxiety... that all heretical depravity should be driven away from the territories of the faithful, we very gladly proclaim and even restate those particular means and methods whereby our Christian endeavor may be fulfilled; since... a zeal for and devotion to our Faith may take hold all the more strongly on the hearts of the faithful.
>
> It has recently come to our attention, not without bitter sorrow, that in some parts of northern Germany... many persons of the Catholic Faith, have abused themselves with devils, *incubi* and *succubi*, and by their incantations, spells, conjurations, and other accursed superstitions and horrid charms, enormities and offences, destroy the offspring of women and the young of cattle, blast and eradicate the fruits of the earth, the grapes of the vine and the fruits of trees. Nay, men and women, beasts of burden, herd beasts, as well as animals of other kinds; also vineyards, orchards, meadows, pastures, corn, wheat, and other cereals of the earth.

When a person became a witch, he or she entered into a pact with Satan to worship him. In making this covenant with the devil, the initiate promised to serve him as Christians promise to serve Christ. Moreover, Satanists had their own liturgy which was a parody of the liturgy said by Roman Catholics. The Italian scholar, Guazzo, listed some of the ancient requirements for becoming a witch:

(1) Denial of the Christian Faith: "I deny the Creator of heaven and earth. I deny my baptism, I deny the worship I formerly paid to God. I adhere to the devil and believe only in thee." Trampling the cross, which accompanied this oath, had been from very early times an important part of the ritual.

(2) Rebaptism by the devil with a new name.

(3) Symbolic removal of the baptismal chrism (the consecrated oil mingled with balm).

(4) Denial of godparents and assigning of new sponsors.

(5) Token surrender to the devil of a piece of clothing.

(6) Swearing allegiance to the devil while standing within a magic circle on the ground.

(7) Request to the devil for their name to be written in the Book of Death.

(8) Promise to sacrifice children to the devil, a step which led to the stories of witches murdering children.

(9) Promise to pay annual tribute to the assigned demon. Only black-coloured gifts were valid.

(10) Marking with the devil's mark in various parts of the body...so that the area marked became insensitive. The mark might vary in shape—a rabbit's foot, a toad, or a spider.

(11) Vows of service to the devil: never to adore the sacrament; to smash holy relics; never to use holy water or candles; and to keep silence on their traffic with Satan (Francesco-Maria Guazzo, *Compendium Maleficarum*, 1608, translated by Dr. R. H. Robbins).

How does one describe a witch? The popular view is that of an ugly old woman riding on a broomstick with a black cat at her side. William West, an English writer during the reign of Elizabeth I, gave the following description of a witch:

Witches: A witch or hag is she who—deluded by a pact made with the devil through his persuasion, inspiration and juggling—thinks she can bring about all manner of evil things, either by thought or imprecation, such as to shake the air with lightnings and thunder, to cause hail and tempests, to remove green corn or trees to another place, to be carried on her familiar spirit (which has taken upon him the deceitful shape of a goat, swine, or calf, etc.) into some mountain far distant, in a wonderfully short space of time, and sometimes to fly upon a staff or fork, or some other instrument, and to spend all the night after with her sweetheart, in playing, sporting, banqueting, dancing, dalliance, and divers other devilish lusts and lewd disports, and to show a thousand such monstrous mockeries (William West, *Simboleography*, 1594).

Another writer described a witch in the following manner:

Witches are those who, because of the magnitude of their crimes, are commonly called *malefici* or evil doers. These witches, by the permission of God, agitate the elements, and disturb the minds of men less trusting in God. Without administering any poison, they kill by the great potency of their charms.... For they summon devils and dare to rouse them so that everyone kills his enemies by evil stratagems. For these witches make use of the blood of victims, and often defile the corpses of the dead.... For the devils are said to love blood, and so when the witches practice the black arts, they mingle blood with water, so that by the color of blood they can more easily conjure up the devils (Gratian, *Decretum*).

Marcello Truzzi describes the traditional initiation into witchcraft:

Basically, witchcraft constitutes a set of beliefs and techniques held in secret which the novice must obtain from someone familiar with them. The normal traditional means for obtaining such information is through another witch who knows these secrets. Traditionally, this can be done through initiation into an existing witch coven or by being told the secrets of the craft by an appropriate relative who is a witch (Marcello Truzzi, "Toward a Sociology of the Occult: Notes on Modern Witchcraft," *Religious Movements in Contemporary America*, ed. by Irving I. Zaretsky and Mark P. Leone, Princeton: Princeton University Press, 1974, p. 636).

Furthermore, these wretches afflict and torment men and women, beasts of burden, herd beasts, as well as cattle of all other kinds, with pain and disease, both internal and external. They hinder men from generating and women from conceiving, whence neither husbands with their wives nor wives with their husbands can perform the sexual act. Above and beyond this, they blasphemously renounce that Faith which they received by the Sacrament of Baptism, and at the instigation of the enemy of the human race they do not shrink from committing and perpetrating the foulest abominations and excesses to the peril of their souls, whereby they offend the Divine Majesty and are a cause of scandal and dangerous example to very many (Papal Bull, *Summis Desiderantes Affectibus 1484*, by Pope Innocent VIII).

The second event which helped cause the great witch hunt was the publication of a book called *Malleus Maleficarum* (Hammer of Witches) in 1486 by Jakob Sprenger and Prior Heinrich Kramer. This publication was a handbook for witch hunters.

The Papal Bull, along with the publication of *Malleus Maleficarum*, led to a witch panic and a 300-year nightmare. People were seeing witches everywhere. Those accused of being witches had little or no defense against their accusers. During this period more than 100,000 people in every European state were executed for supposedly being witches. The brutal methods of the inquisitors is summed up by R. H. Robbins:

(1) The accused was presumed guilty until he had proved his innocence. The inquisition adopted this pivot of Roman Imperial law; but in matters of belief, vindication was almost impossible.

(2) Suspicion, gossip, or denunciation was sufficient indication of guilt to hail a person before the Inquisition.

(3) To justify the activity of the Inquisition, the offence, whatever it might have been, was correlated with heresy. Thus, the men who killed the bigoted Inquisitor Peter Partyr in 1252 were tried not for murder but for heresy (as opponents of the Inquisition).

(4) Witnesses were not identified. Often their accusations were not made known to the defendant. In 1254 Pope Innocent IV granted accusers anonymity.

(5) Witnesses disallowed in other offences were encouraged

to inform against heretics, convicted perjurers, persons without civil rights, children of tender years, and ex-communicates (including condemned heretics). If a hostile witness retracted his evidence, he was prosecuted for perjury, but his testimony was allowed to stand. However, according to the Inquisitor Nicholas Eymeric (1360), if the retraction was less favourable to the accused, the judged could accept this second testimony.

(6) No witnesses were allowed to testify on behalf of the accused; nor was his previous good reputation as a citizen or Christian taken into account.

(7) The accused was permitted no counsel, since the lawyer would thereby be guilty of defending heresy. (For a short time lawyers had been allowed, especially when inquisitors were sitting on Episcopal courts, and this privilege was resumed in the 17th century.)....

(9) The judges were encouraged to trick the accused into confession. The Inquisitor Sylvestor Prierias in 1521 told how this could be done.

(10) Although technically allowed only as a last resort, the practice of torture was regularly used, and could be inflicted on any witness. Civil authorities employed torture, but the Inquisition extended and systematized its use. Torture had been sanctioned as a means to discover heresy by Pope Innocent IV in 1257, in a Bull *Ad extirpanda*, and was confirmed by later popes; it was not abolished until 1816 by Pope Pius VII....

(14) Generally no appeal was countenanced. (R. H. Robbins, *The Encyclopedia of Witchcraft and Demonology*, New York: Crown Publ., 1959, p. 180).

The Power of Witches

Witches were supposed to have a variety of different powers which kept the people in fear of them. They supposedly could cast spells which would raise storms, magically destroy crops and turn themselves into werewolves and vampires. However, the most feared power thought to be held by the witches was that of bewitchment, the ability to cause sickness and death.

Roger Hart makes an apt comment:

It can easily be imagined how — in the days when medicine was primitive — various ailments could be mistaken for bewitchment; paralysis, lockjaw, fevers, anemia, sclerosis, epilepsy, hysteria. Such illnesses often displayed symptoms which were extremely frightening to educated and uneducated people alike (Hart, *Witchcraft*, op. cit., p. 54).

To this list we could add Huntington's Chorea and Tourette's Syndrome. Huntington's Chorea is a disease which does not show up in most of its victims until they are past 30 years of age. This disease causes the victim to behave in a peculiar manner, including involuntary body movements, fits of anger and irritability and a loss of intelligence.

The victim may make strange outbursts of laughter, cry like a baby or talk endlessly. It can easily be seen how a sufferer could be mistaken for being bewitched or being a witch. Huntington's Chorea is also an inherited disease which would convince the superstitious that the bewitchment has been passed to the children.

Tourette's Syndrome is a rare disease which usually begins in childhood. The victim experiences tics — involuntary muscle movements — throughout the body but especially in the face. The sufferer also may kick and stamp his feet. Along with making awful faces, the victim makes involuntary noises which include shouts, grunts and swearing. All of these symptoms are beyond the control of the sufferer but appear to the uneducated as a sign of being a witch, possessed by the devil.

Many today still consider victims of such diseases as demon possessed or oppressed. Research funding into such rare diseases has lagged far behind that of the major prevalent diseases of our day. Such "orphan" diseases (so named because medical and pharmaceutical interests do not want to fund research on obscure diseases whose treatment would not be profitable financially) will probably remain largely uninvestigated until comprehensive research can be funded. However, the little we do know about these diseases leads us to conclude absolutely that one should not be blamed for demonic involvement when he is in reality the victim of a truly physiological aberration.

Salem Witch Trials

America did not escape the great witch hunt. Roger Hart comments on the Salem witch trials:

Perhaps no single witch hunt has attracted so much popular

attention as that which took place at Salem in New England in the year 1692. This American witch hunt was remarkable not merely on account of the large number of people found guilty (Salem was a small community), but also because of the late date at which it took place. No one had been executed for witchcraft in England, for example, since 1684. But above all, the Salem affair has generally been seen as a fascinating microcosm of the whole Western witchcraft delusion (Ibid, p. 109).

Although Salem was a relatively small town of about 100 households, the percentage of those tried for being witches was enormous. As historian R. H. Robbins reports:

All in all, the toll of Salem, a township of a hundred-odd households, was enormous. During the hysteria, almost 150 people were arrested. A search of all the court records would no doubt add to this number. Because of the time taken to convict each prisoner, only thirty-one were tried in 1692, not including Sarah Churchill and Mary Warren, two accusers who briefly recanted. The court of Oyer and Terminer (hear and determine) sentenced to death all thirty-one, of whom six were men. Nineteen were hanged. Of the remaining twelve, two (Sarah Osborne and Anne Foster) died in jail; one (Giles Cory) was pressed to death; one (Tituba) was held indefinitely in jail without trial. Two (Abigail Faulkner and Elizabeth Proctor) postponed execution by pleading pregnancy and lived long enough to be reprieved. One (Mary Bradbury) escaped from jail after sentencing; and five made confessions which secured reprieves for them (Robbins, op. cit., p. 185).

Fourteen years later one of the accusers, Anne Putnam, retracted her charges, stating she and others carried the guilt of innocent blood.

Comment on Witch Hunting

The great witch hunt of the Middle Ages is remarkable for a number of reasons. First, it is remarkable because it lasted some 300 years and took hundreds of thousands of lives. It is also remarkable because it took place during a time of renewed interest in learning.

The people who participated in this craze were not all irrational individuals but were rather some of the most brilliantly educated people of that day. Scientists, philosophers and lawyers were among those who participated in the great witch hunt, showing that superstition knows no educational bounds.

It is also unfortunate that much of the persecution came from professing Christians doing it in the Name of God. The passages which were used to justify the witch hunt were misread and taken totally out of context. The legal penalties of such Old Testament crimes were part of the then-operating theocracy in Israel.

The Lord God was the King in Israel; He had the right to determine the crimes and punishments against His holy and sovereign state. One who participated in witchcraft was aligning himself with Satan, the foe of God. Such an alignment was treason against the government of Israel, a government directed personally by the Lord God.

Even today treason is often punished by death. However, since no nation today is a theocracy, a nation governed directly by God, the penalties instituted then are not applicable. Witchcraft is still evil and is still rebellion against God. It is not treason. Jesus Christ warned that physical death was not the ultimate punishment anyway.

Those who practice witchcraft, displaying their rejection of Jesus Christ, should heed His warning: "And do not fear those who kill the body, but are unable to kill the soul; but rather fear Him who is able to destroy soul and body in hell" (Matthew 10:28, NASB).

Witchcraft Today

Although witch hunting and witch trials no longer occur, the practice of witchcraft continues. The modern witch does not fit the stereotype of the old hag, for many people who are practicing this art are in the mainstream of society. The question is why? Why a renewed interest in this ancient art among both the educated and the ignorant? Daniel Cohen lists a couple of possible reasons:

> First, there is the eternal appeal of magic, the promise, however muted, that there are secrets available that will give a person power, money, love, and all those things he or she desires but cannot seem to obtain. Second, witchcraft is a put-down and a revolt against some of the establishment beliefs in organized religion, science, and rational thinking. The historic connection between witchcraft and drugs and

sex also has undoubted appeal. Here is a set of beliefs that claim to be part of an extremely ancient religion. Yet this is a religion in which drugs and free sexuality are not condemned, but might be encouraged. Despite all the publicity and all the witch covens that have been organized, witchcraft still is not taken seriously (Daniel Cohen, *A Natural History of Unnatural Things*, New York: McCall Pub. Co., 1971, pp. 31, 32).

Modern witchcraft bears little resemblance to the witchcraft of the Middle Ages or to witchcraft in still primitive, preliterate societies. Modern witchcraft is a relatively recent development (the last 200 years), embraces hundreds of beliefs and practices and has hundreds of thousands of adherents. The one common theme running through modern witchcraft is the practice of and belief in things forbidden by God in the Bible as occultic.

Up until a couple of decades ago, and for previous centuries, there were no admitted witches anywhere. Most people have thought of witchcraft as something that only the superstitious gave any credence to. Witch hunts and broomsticks were filed away together in a little-used corner of the mind.

Today, in a massive spin-off from the culture-wide interest in the occult, this has all changed. Tens of thousands across America—some of them with university degrees—are dabbling in witchcraft, Satanism, voodoo, and other forms of black and white magic. Witches appear openly on television. Every high school is said to have its own witch. In Cleveland you can rent a witch to liven up a party. There are some 80,000 persons practicing white magic in the United States, with 6,000 in Chicago alone.

Some of this is a fad. But unfortunately, much of it isn't. Murder after murder has been linked to the craze, with the murderers openly admitting to police or to reporters that they worshipped Satan. Police, more and more frequently are finding grim evidence of both animal and human sacrifice (George Vandeman, *Psychic Roulette*, Nashville, TN: Thomas Nelson, Inc., 1973, pp. 99, 100).

Witchcraft is not dead today as can be observed by an article appearing in the *Los Angeles Times* concerning the goddess movement:

...Eerie monotones...reverberated on the UC Santa Cruz campus. Cheers and whoops went up for the goddesses of yore—Isis, Astara, Demeter, Artemis, etc.

184

...The event was indicative of a burgeoning spiritual dimension to the women's liberation movement in America....

Christine Downing, head of San Diego State University's religious studies department, estimates that many—if not most—spiritually sensitive women in the women's movement are willing to replace the biblical God with a frankly pagan and polytheistic approach.

Witchcraft is aiding the women in their search for roots and rituals—without the connotations of evil usually associated with witchcraft.

A Santa Cruz woman...said, "Some of the women think of themselves as witches, but not all."

A brief, unscheduled appearance—met with enthusiastic applause—was made by Z Budapest. A self-described witch...the goddess movement knows her more as a leader of the Susan B. Anthony Coven No. 1 in Los Angeles and a charismatic spokeswoman for a feminist brand of Wicca, an ancient women's religion (witchcraft).

The goddess movement, also called the women-spirit movement, apparently considers its first major gathering to have been a conference attended by about 1,200 women at the University of Massachusetts in late 1975....

The ancient Mediterranean world, pagan Europe, Native America and Hindu tradition are all sources for goddess imagery....

A religious phenomenon virtually unknown outside feminist circles, "goddess consciousness" will be widely known in three to five years (*Los Angeles Times*, April 10, 1978).

The Bible and Witchcraft

Both the Old and New Testaments make repeated references to the practice of witchcraft and sorcery, and whenever these practices are referred to they are always condemned by God. The Bible condemns all forms of witchcraft, including sorcery, astrology and reading human and animal entrails. The following passages describe the various forms of witchcraft which are condemned by God.

You shall not allow a sorceress to live (Exodus 22:18, NASB).

You shall not eat anything with the blood, nor practice divination or soothsaying (Leviticus 19:26, NASB).

Do not turn to mediums or spiritists; do not seek them out

to be defiled by them. I am the Lord your God (Leviticus 19:31, NASB).

Now a man or a woman who is a medium or a spiritist shall surely be put to death. They shall be stoned with stones, their bloodguiltiness is upon them (Leviticus 20:27, NASB).

You shall not behave thus toward the Lord your God, for every abominable act which the Lord hates they have done for their gods; for they even burn their sons and daughters in the fire to their gods (Deuteronomy 12:31, NASB).

There shall not be found among you anyone who makes his son or his daughter pass through the fire, one who uses divination, one who practices witchcraft, or one who interprets omens, or a sorcerer, or one who casts a spell, or a medium, or a spiritist, or one who calls up the dead.... For those nations, which you shall dispossess, listen to those who practice witchcraft and to diviners, but as for you, the Lord your God has not allowed you to do so (Deuteronomy 18:10, 11, 14, NASB).

For rebellion is as the sin of divination, and insubordination is as iniquity and idolatry. Because you have rejected the word of the Lord, He has also rejected you from being king (1 Samuel 15:23, NASB).

Then they made their sons and their daughters pass through the fire, and practiced divination and enchantments, and sold themselves to do evil in the sight of the Lord, provoking Him (2 Kings 17:17, NASB).

And he made his son pass through the fire, practiced witchcraft and used divination, and dealt with mediums and spiritists. He did much evil in the sight of the Lord provoking Him to anger (2 Kings 21:6, NASB).

Moreover, Josiah removed the mediums, and the spiritists and teraphim and the idols and all the abominations that were seen in the land of Judah and in Jerusalem, that he might confirm the words of the law which were written in the book that Hilkiah the priest found in the house of the Lord (2 Kings 23:24, NASB).

So Saul died for his trespass which he committed against the Lord, because of the word of the Lord which he did not keep; and also because he asked counsel of a medium, making inquiry of it, and did not inquire of the Lord. Therefore He killed him, and turned the kingdom to David the son of Jesse (1 Chronicles 10:13, NASB).

And when they say to you, "Consult the mediums and the spiritists who whisper and mutter," should not a people consult their God? Should they consult the dead on behalf of the living? (Isaiah 8:19, NASB).

Then the spirit of the Egyptians will be demoralized within them; and I will confound their strategy, so that they will resort to idols and ghosts of the dead, and to mediums and spiritists (Isaiah 19:3, NASB).

Stand fast now in your spells and in your many sorceries with which you have labored from your youth; perhaps you will be able to profit, perhaps you may cause trembling. You are wearied with your many counsels; let now the astrologers, those who prophesy by the stars, those who predict by the new moons, stand up and save you from what will come upon you (Isaiah 47:12, 13, NASB).

But as for you, do not listen to your prophets, your diviners, your dreamers, your soothsayers, or your sorcerers, who speak to you, saying, "You shall not serve the king of Babylon." For they prophesy a lie to you, in order to remove you far from your land; and I will drive you out, and you will perish (Jeremiah 27:9, 10, NASB).

"Then I will draw near to you for judgment; and I will be a swift witness against the sorcerers and against the adulterers and against those who swear falsely, and against those who oppress the wage earner in his wages, the widow and the orphan, and those who turn aside the alien, and do not fear Me," says the Lord of Hosts (Malachi 3:5, NASB).

And when they had gone through the whole island as far as Paphos, they found a certain magician, a Jewish false prophet whose name was Bar-Jesus, who was with the proconsul, Sergius Paulus, a man of intelligence. This man summoned Barnabas and Saul and sought to hear the word of God. But Elymas the magician (for thus his name is translated) was opposing them, seeking to turn the proconsul away from the faith. But Saul, who was also known as Paul, filled with the Holy Spirit, fixed his gaze upon him, and said, "You who are full of all deceit and fraud, you son of the devil, you enemy of all righteousness, will you not cease to make crooked the straight ways of the Lord?" (Acts 13:6-10, NASB).

Now the deeds of the flesh are evident, which are: immorality, impurity, sensuality, idolatry, sorcery, enmities, strife, jealousy, outbursts of anger, disputes, dissensions, factions, envying, drunkenness, carousing, and things like these, of which I forewarn you just as I have forewarned you that those who practice such things shall not inherit the kingdom of God (Galatians 5:19-21, NASB).

But for the cowardly and unbelieving and abominable and murderers and immoral persons and sorcerers and idolaters and all liars, their part will be in the lake that burns with fire and brimstone, which is the second death (Revelation 21:8, NASB).

CHAPTER TWENTY-THREE

Conclusion

The existence of an evil, supernatural realm, led by Satan and supported by his legions of demons, is a reality. Satan's devices are many, and his methods are as varied as his devices. We as believers never are called to investigate all of these occult phenomena. Preoccupation with Satan's methods is not the best means of approaching our foe, our enemy, the accuser of the brethren. However, this does not mean we are to do nothing.

Rather, as believers, we are exhorted in three major areas. First, we are called to *understand* — understand that Satan has already been defeated. Christ's death and resurrection sealed Satan's fate and destruction. That fact became reality for us when we trusted Christ.

Second, we are called to *know* — know Satan's strategy. Not to know all his methods, but rather his means of operation. This includes his being disguised as an angel of light. Satan's *modus operandi*, aside from a direct assault of lies, also includes the more subtle and often used art of deception. He seeks to lure through the things of the world and the tempations of the flesh. Satan's desire is to replace God's plan with his counterfeit, just as he attempted to do in the Garden of Eden.

Third, besides having a good defense of knowing our position in Christ and recognizing Satan's strategy, we must *be on the offensive* in what we do. This means knowing God and making Him known. When we get closer to our

Lord and share the gospel with others, it pierces Satan as with a knife — the Lord uses us to advance His Kingdom and bring Satan's domain to ruin. For our mastery over Satan is not in our power, but in God's power and through His plan — sharing the gospel. This is why Jesus said in Luke that we should not rejoice because we have power over demons but because our names are in the book of life (Luke 10:17-20).

Paul clearly states, "For I am not ashamed of the gospel, for it is the power of God for salvation to everyone who believes" (Romans 1:16 NASB). Communicating the gospel *is* our goal, even amid all the conflicts that Satan and the world attempt to throw at us. The command to believers is to grow in the gospel and to share it with others.

This is graphically and clearly illustrated in chapter six of Paul's epistle to the Ephesians. The whole point of this chapter is often overlooked, as the emphasis is usually placed on the "armor of God." That is not Paul's point. The whole reason for Paul's emphasis on the armor to stand against the powers of darkness is the need to get the gospel out (Ephesians 6:18-20 NASB).

In this section, Ephesians 6:10-20, Paul points out that the true battle stems from the evil forces in the heavenlies, and that his purpose for life is to spread the gospel. His very prayer at the end of the book, which comes in the context of this section on the armor of God, is for him to be able to *make known the gospel*. He places that prayer there by design and not by accident. As Paul saw fit to end his discussion of the forces of darkness in that way, so do we:

> Finally, be strong in the Lord, and in the strength of His might. Put on the full armor of God, that you may be able to stand firm against the schemes of the devil. For our struggle is not against flesh and blood, but against the rulers, against the powers, against the world forces of this darkness, against the spiritual forces of wickedness in the heavenly places. Therefore take up the full armor of God, that you may be able to resist in the evil day, and having done everything to stand firm. Stand firm therefore, having girded your loins with truth, and having put on the breastplate of righteousness, and having shod your feet with the preparation of the gospel of peace; in addition to all, taking up the shield of faith with

which you will be able to extinguish all the flaming missiles of the evil one. And take the helmet of salvation, and the sword of the Spirit, which is the word of God. With all prayer and petition pray at all times in the Spirit, and with this in view, be on the alert with all perseverance and petition for all the saints, and pray on my behalf, that utterance may be given to me in the opening of my mouth, to make known with boldness the mystery of the gospel, for which I am an ambassador in chains; that in proclaiming it I may speak boldly, as I ought to speak (Ephesians 6:10-20 NASB).

Magic and the Occult in Literature

Many Christians have legitimate questions about the use of fairies, witches, goblins, etc., in literature, and what should be our Christian response. Should we enjoy and condone writings which elevate supernatural powers only related to the God of the Bible? What of Gandalf in Tolkien's *Lord of the Rings?* Or of Galadriel and the palintir? What of C. S. Lewis, G. K. Chesterton or even Superman?

Another question arises. Should Christians celebrate Halloween? This type of question is so commonly asked by Christians, and deals with the ramifications of the occult on such a practical level, we thought it should be addressed.

Literature

Some believe that literature which elevates beings of supernatural powers should not be accepted and read by Christians. The literature is often accused of condoning such occultic practices as white magic — magic used for good purposes.

However, this is not the case. First, although white magic is sometimes used for the good, its foundation is usually the world of nature without God. The true God through Christ is never their basis for supernatural power. Behind the world of fairies in Lewis, Tolkien and others is a Supreme Being of good, and often some type of lesser but superpowerful being of evil, who is manifested in various ways, but usually defeated by the Good.

The second issue is that of motive. The literature often seeks to honor and promote values associated with the attributes of the God found in Scripture, such as love, justice, truth, and faith in a trustworthy object. White magic does not have this objective. There is a vast difference between the supernatural in literature and white magic both in purpose and in practice.

Dr. John Warwick Montgomery, one of the few Christian authors to address this important topic, and one who is well-qualified because of his interest and expertise in this area, offers this excellent analysis:

> Like Tarot symbolism, the imagery of Faerie strikes to the archetypal level, thus driving us closer to Christ or leaving us in hatred or despair. Samuel Roberts, a noted Welsh scholar, said that he "believed such things (fairies) existed and that God allowed them to appear in times of great ignorance to convince people of the existence of an invisible world." It is in this spirit that C. S. Lewis, by way of his seven Narnian Chronicles, and J. R. R. Tolkien, in *The Hobbit*, *The Lord of the Rings*, and his short stories ("Leap by Niggle," "Farmer Giles of Ham," etc.), have employed the motifs of Faerie to bring sensitive readers to face spiritual reality—archetypally in their own souls and factually in terms of the "existence of an invisible world" (John W. Montgomery, *Principalities and Powers*, Minneapolis, MN: Bethany Fellowship, 1973, p. 136).

Participation in Halloween

The history of Halloween has already been discussed, but the celebration of it has not. What should a Christian's attitude be toward this occasion? This is an often-asked, practical question involving one aspect of the occult.

Halloween has held an association with the occult throughout its history, and to a degree that stigma still exists today. While we don't feel that any hard and fast rules should be made about participation in Halloween festivities, we do feel that people, especially parents, should use discretion in regulating their degree of involvement. Rather than totally ignoring this occasion we would encourage Christians to develop creative alternatives to the traditional Halloween celebration.

The guiding principle from Scripture concerning areas that are not directly addressed is found in Paul's statement, "Let every man be fully persuaded in his own mind" (Romans 14:5 NASB). In other words, whatever you do, do not violate your conscience. If you are not sure you — or your children — should participate in an activity such as Halloween, then you should not enter into it. Your judgment in these areas must be guided by the Holy Spirit.

The Authority
of the Believer

A t the center of the occult, either openly or disguised as an "angel of light," is Satan. Peter exhorts believers concerning our chief foe when he writes, "Be of sober spirit, be on the alert. Your adversary, the devil, prowls about like a roaring lion, seeking someone to devour" (1 Peter 5:8, NASB).

Christians often have the tendency to "blame it all on the devil," when in fact it was their own carelessness or fleshly nature which led to the sin or error. It can also be said, however, that even when it is our fleshly nature or the world which draws us from the Lord—and not the devil directly—it is nevertheless true that Satan and his army of demons desire that we be drawn to the world's standards.

Satan is the one who ultimately desires that we pursue the lusts of the flesh, and it is he who sits as the "god of this world" (Ephesians 2:1-10). Though not always directly involved, Satan's prime objective is the defeat of God, and for us that means our defeat.

The authority of the believer spells out the authority a believer has over Satan and his efforts to thwart God's desire for our lives and his attempt to defeat us.

For the rest of your life, one of the most important Scriptural messages you'll ever consider is found here.

As you study the Old Testament, you see that men and women were in a constant struggle with Satan, fighting many spiritual battles. As you study the life of Christ, and Paul, and the other Apostles, you see a constant spiritual struggle. Christians today face many spiritual battles.

I'm so glad I learned the authority of the believer before I went to South America. The authority of the believer is a possession that belongs to every true child of God. And it gives so much authority over the enemy that Satan has tried to blind most believers to the authority they have.

During Easter week at Balboa, I first learned of the authority of the believer. About 50,000 high school and college students came down for Easter. With André Kole, the illusionist, we packed out a big ballroom several nights in a row—for two or three meetings a night. So many people were coming to our meetings, in fact, that many of the bars were empty. It really irritated some of the people. The second night, one of the men from a night club came over to break up our meeting. They figured if they broke up one of them, that would finish it for us.

As André was performing, this guy pulled up with his Dodge Dart all souped up. With a deafening sound, he popped the clutch and went roaring down the street. Everyone inside, of course, turned around and looked out to see the commotion. Finally, André got them settled down.

Then the guy went around the block again. As he stopped out front, he revved it up again and roared down the street. By this time everyone was whispering and wondering what was going on. Some stood up, trying to look out the window.

When the guy went back around the block again, I knew that if he repeated his performance one more time, it would break up the meeting. Turning to Gene Huntsman, one of our staff members, I said, "I think Satan is trying to break up this meeting. Let's step out in the doorway and exercise the authority of the believer." So we stepped out and prayed a very simple prayer.

When the guy came back, he started to rev it up again, and as he popped the clutch—pow! The rear end of his car blew all over the street. By that time, we just thanked the Lord and went over and pushed him off the street. As I shared the *Four Spiritual Laws* with him, it reminded me that Jesus said all authority is given to the believer in heaven and in earth.

Now, to point out what the authority is, let's look at Luke 10:19: "Behold, I give unto you power to tread on serpents and scorpions, and over all the power of the enemy: and nothing shall by any means hurt you" (KJV). Two separate Greek words are used for *power* here, but one English translation. The first one should be translated *authority*, not *power*. The Lord is saying, "Behold, I give you authority over the power of the enemy." The Christian does not have *power* over Satan; he has *authority* over Satan. Let me give you an illustration.

I used to live in Argentina. Buenos Aires, the second largest city in the western hemisphere, has six subway lines, one of the longest streets in the world—almost 60 miles long, and one of the widest streets in the world—25 lanes, almost three blocks wide. One street is called Corrente, which means *current*. It is a solid current of traffic—sometimes considered one of the longest parking lots in the world.

One intersection is so busy, about the only way you can make it across is to confess any unknown sin, make sure you are filled with the Spirit, commit your life to the Lord and dash madly! But one day we approached, and an amazing thing took place.

Out in the center of the intersection was a platform, on which stood a uniformed policeman. About 20 of us waited at the corner to cross. All of a sudden, he blew his whistle and put up his hand. As he lifted his hand, all those cars came to a screeching halt. With all of his personal power he couldn't have stopped one of those cars, but he had something far better; he was invested with the authority of the police department. And the moving cars and the pedestrians recognized that authority. So, first, we see that authority is delegated power.

Second, let's examine the source of this authority. Paul writes, "And what is the surpassing greatness of His Power toward us who believe. These are in accordance with the working of the strength of His might which He brought about in Christ, when He raised Him from the dead, and seated Him at His right hand in the heavenly places, far above all rule and authority and power and dominion, and every name that is named, not only in this age, but also in the one to come. And He put all things in subjection under His feet, and gave Him as head over all things to the Church, which is His Body, the fullness of Him who fills all in all" (Ephesians 1:19-23, NASB).

When Jesus Christ was raised from the dead, we see the act of the resurrection and the surrounding events as one of the greatest workings of God manifested in the Scriptures. So powerful was the omnipotency of God that the Holy Spirit, through the Apostle Paul, used four different words for power.

First, the greatness of his power—in the Greek—is *dunamis*, from which comes the English word *dynamite*. Then comes the word *working—energios*, where *energy* comes from—a working manifestation or activity. The third word is *strength—kratous—*meaning to *exercise strength*. Then comes *might*, or *esquai—*a great summation of power.

These four words signify that behind the events described in Ephesians 1:19-23 are the greatest workings of God manifested in the Scriptures—even greater than creation. This great unleashing of God's might involved the resurrection, the ascension and the seating of Jesus Christ. "When He had disarmed the rulers and authorities, He made a public display of them, having triumphed over them through Him" (Colossians 2:15, NASB). Satan was defeated and disarmed. All of this unleashing of God's might in the resurrection, the ascension and the seating of Jesus Christ was for you and me—that we might gain victory right now over Satan. The source of our authority over Satan is rooted in God and His power.

Third, what are the qualifications you must have to be able to be consistent in exercising the authority of the believer?

First, there must be knowledge, a knowledge of our position in Christ and of Satan's defeat. At the moment of salvation we are elevated to a heavenly placement. We don't have to climb some ladder of faith to get there. We are immediately identified in the eyes of God—and of Satan—with Christ's crucifixion and burial, and we are co-resurrected, co-ascended and co-seated with Jesus Christ at the right hand of the Father, far above all rule and

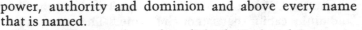

power, authority and dominion and above every name that is named.

The problem is that, though both God and Satan are aware of this, most believers are not. And if you don't understand who you are, you will never exercise that authority which is the birthright of every true believer in Jesus. So the first step is knowledge.

The second qualification is belief. A lot of people really don't comprehend one of the primary aspects of belief, which is "to live in accordance with." This is not merely mental assent, but it leads to action. You could say it like this: That which the mind accepts, the will obeys. Otherwise you are not really a true believer. Do we actually believe that we've been co-resurrected, co-ascended, co-seated with Jesus Christ? If we do, our actions will be fervent.

We should wake up each morning and say, "Lord, I accept my position. I acknowledge it to be at the right hand of the Father, and today, through the Holy Spirit, cause it to be a reality to me, that I might experience victory." You talk about space walking! A Christian who is filled with the Holy Spirit and who knows his position with Christ is walking in the heavenlies. I put it this way: Before you can be any earthly good, you have to be heavenly minded. Your mind should be set at the right hand of the Father, knowing who you are.

Often, when I wake up in the morning, while my eyes are still closed, I go over my position in Christ, thanking the Holy Spirit for indwelling me, etc. But every morning, I acknowledge my position in Christ. I don't have to drum it up—I ask the Holy Spirit to make my position real in my experience.

The third qualification is humility. While belief introduces us to our place of throne power at the right hand of the Father, only humility will ensure that we can exercise that power continuously. Let me tell you, ever since Mr. and Mrs. Adam occupied the garden of Eden, man has needed to be reminded of his limitations. Even regenerated man thinks he can live without seriously considering his total dependence upon God.

Yet, humility to me is not going around saying, "I'm nothing, I'm nothing, I'm nothing. I'm just the dirt under the toenail. When I get to heaven all I want is that little old dinky cabin, that's enough for me." That's an insult to Christ. It's not humility—it's pride. Humility is knowing who you are and knowing who made you who you are and giving Him the glory for it. Sometimes, when I hear a person claim he's nothing, I say, "Look sir, I don't know about you, but I'm someone." I *am* someone. On December 19, 1959, at 8:30 at night, Jesus Christ made me a child of God, and I'm sure not going to say I'm nothing. Maybe I'm not all I should be, but I am more than I used to be, and God's not finished with me yet. I know He has made me, and I won't insult what God has made.

The next qualification, the fourth one, is boldness. Humility allows the greatest boldness. True boldness is faith in full manifestation. When God has spoken and you hold back, that is not faith, it is sin. We need men and women who have set their minds at the right hand of the Father and who fear no one but God. True boldness comes from realizing your position in Jesus Christ and being filled with the Holy Spirit.

The fifth and final qualification is awareness, a realization that being at the right hand of the Father also puts you in the place of the most intense spiritual conflict. The moment your eyes are open to the fact that you are in that place, that you have been co-resurrected, co-ascended and co-seated with Christ, Satan will do everything he possibly can to wipe you out, to discourage you. You become a marked individual. The last thing Satan wants is a Spirit-filled believer who knows his throne rights. Satan will start working in your life to cause you not to study or appropriate the following principles which show you how to defeat him.

Going through all of the above was necessary to lay a foundation on which you can exercise the authority of the believer. Here is how I do it. Remember, authority is delegated power. Usually I speak right out loud and address Satan directly, "Satan, in the name of the Lord Jesus Christ..." I always use this point first because those three names—Lord, Jesus and Christ—describe His crucifixion, burial, resurrection and seating, and His victory over Satan. "Satan, in the name of the Lord Jesus Christ and His shed blood on the cross, I command you to stop your activities in this area." Or, "Satan, in the name of the Lord Jesus Christ and His shed blood on the cross, I acknowledge that the victory is Jesus' and all honor and glory in this situation go to Him." I speak to Satan in various ways, but I always use those beginning phrases because they remind him that he is already defeated.

Next, I realize there is nothing I can do. I have no power over Satan, I only have authority. And the more I learn of the power behind me, the force behind me, the greater boldness I have in exercising the authority of the believer.

Once the authority of the believer is exercised, though, we must be patient. Never have I exercised that authority that I did not see Satan defeated, but I have had to learn to wait.

Some time ago, for example, I was to speak in a university in South America. Because of the university's Marxist leanings, I was the first American to speak there in four years, and it was a tense situation. Big photographs of me had been posted all over campus and the Communist students, trying to influence the other students to stay away from the meeting, had painted "CIA Agent" in red letters across the posters. I thought CIA meant "Christ in Action." Anyway, it backfired. Most of the students had never seen a CIA agent, so they came to the meeting to see what one looked like, and the room was packed. However, as is often the case when someone speaks in that part of the world, professional Marxist agitators had also come, and their intent was to disrupt the meeting.

When I go to another country I like to speak as well as possible in the language of that country. So I pointed out to the audience that I was learning their language and that night I would be lecturing in it. Well, I started, and, oh, it was horrible! My back was against the wall—the chairs were about five inches from me. And one after another, these agitators would jump up and throw accusations at me, call me "a filthy pig," etc., and hurl words at me that I didn't even know. Right in front of the audience they twisted me around their little fingers. I couldn't answer them; I didn't even know what they were saying. I felt so sorry for the Christians who were there because they had looked forward so eagerly to my coming to the campus and to seeing people come to Christ.

After 45 minutes of this heckling, I just felt like crying. I literally wanted to crawl under the carpet. My wife asked me one time, "Honey, what's the darkest situation you've ever been in?" And I said, "It was that one."

By this time I was ready to give up. Every time I even mentioned the name of Jesus they laughed. I had exercised the authority of the believer, and now I thought, "God, why aren't you doing something? Why? Isn't Satan defeated?" Well, I wasn't walking by faith. You see, God works when it brings the greatest honor and glory to His name, not to ours.

Finally, God started to work. The secretary of the Revolutionary Student Movement stood up, and everyone else became silent. I figured she must be someone important.

She was quite an outspoken woman, and I didn't know what to expect. But this is what she said. "Mr. McDowell, if I become a Christian tonight, will God give me the love for people that you have shown for us?"

Well, I don't have to tell you what happened. It broke just about everyone's heart who was there, and we had 58 decisions for Christ.

I've learned to exercise the authority of the believer and then to walk by faith and to wait. Sometimes I have had to wait six months or a year, but in the long run, when I look back on a situation and see how God has been glorified, it is beautiful.

And I never repeat the exercise of the authority of the believer in a given situation. Satan only needs one warning. God will take care of it from there. Jesus said, "All authority has been given to me in heaven and earth. Go therefore, and make disciples of all nations."

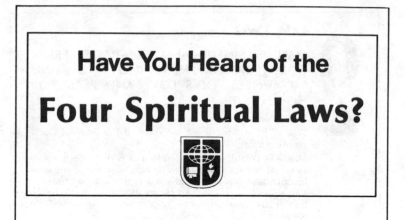

Have You Heard of the

Four Spiritual Laws?

1

Just as there are physical laws that govern the physical universe, so are there spiritual laws which govern your relationship with God.

LAW ONE

GOD **LOVES** YOU, AND OFFERS A WONDERFUL **PLAN** FOR YOUR LIFE.

(References contained in this booklet should be read in context from the Bible wherever possible.)

God's Love

"For God so loved the world, that He gave His only begotten Son, that whoever believes in Him should not perish, but have eternal life" (John 3:16).

God's Plan

(Christ speaking) "I came that they might have life, and might have it abundantly" (that it might be full and meaningful) (John 10:10).

Why is it that most people are not experiencing the abundant life? Because . . .

LAW TWO

MAN IS **SINFUL** AND **SEPARATED** FROM GOD. THEREFORE, HE CANNOT KNOW AND EXPERIENCE GOD'S LOVE AND PLAN FOR HIS LIFE.

Man Is Sinful

"For all have sinned and fall short of the glory of God" (Romans 3:23).

Man was created to have fellowship with God; but, because of his stubborn self-will, he chose to go his own independent way and fellowship with God was broken. This self-will, characterized by an attitude of active rebellion or passive indifference, is evidence of what the Bible calls sin.

Man Is Separated

"For the wages of sin is death" (spiritual separation from God) (Romans 6:23).

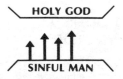

This diagram illustrates that God is holy and man is sinful. A great gulf separates the two. The arrows illustrate that man is continually trying to reach God and the abundant life through his own efforts, such as a good life, philosophy or religion.

The third law explains the only way to bridge this gulf . . .

LAW THREE

JESUS CHRIST IS GOD'S **ONLY** PROVISION FOR MAN'S SIN. THROUGH HIM YOU CAN KNOW AND EXPERIENCE GOD'S LOVE AND PLAN FOR YOUR LIFE.

He Died in Our Place

"But God demonstrates His own love toward us, in that while we were yet sinners, Christ died for us" (Romans 5:8).

He Rose from the Dead

"Christ died for our sins . . . He was buried . . . He was raised on the third day, according to the Scriptures . . . He appeared to Peter, then to the twelve. After that He appeared to more than five hundred . . ." (I Corinthians 15:3-6).

He Is the Only Way to God

"Jesus said to him, 'I am the way, and the truth, and the life; no one comes to the Father, but through Me' " (John 14:6).

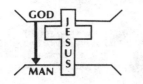

This diagram illustrates that God has bridged the gulf which separates us from Him by sending His Son, Jesus Christ, to die on the cross in our place to pay the penalty for our sins.

It is not enough just to know these three laws . . .

LAW FOUR

WE MUST INDIVIDUALLY **RECEIVE** JESUS CHRIST AS SAVIOR AND LORD; THEN WE CAN KNOW AND EXPERIENCE GOD'S LOVE AND PLAN FOR OUR LIVES.

We Must Receive Christ

"But as many as received Him, to them He gave the right to become children of God, even to those who believe in His name" (John 1:12).

We Receive Christ Through Faith

"For by grace you have been saved through faith; and that not of yourselves, it is the gift of God; not as a result of works, that no one should boast" (Ephesians 2:8,9).

When We Receive Christ, We Experience a New Birth.
(Read John 3:1-8.)

We Receive Christ by Personal Invitation

(Christ is speaking): "Behold, I stand at the door and knock; if any one hears My voice and opens the door, I will come in to him" (Revelation 3:20).

Receiving Christ involves turning to God from self (repentance) and trusting Christ to come into our lives to forgive our sins and to make us the kind of people He wants us to be. Just to agree intellectually that Jesus Christ is the Son of God and that He died on the cross for our sins is not enough. Nor is it enough to have an emotional experience. We receive Jesus Christ by faith, as an act of the will.

These two circles represent two kinds of lives:

SELF-DIRECTED LIFE
S — Self is on the throne
† — Christ is outside the life
• — Interests are directed by self, often resulting in discord and frustration

CHRIST-DIRECTED LIFE
† — Christ is in the life and on the throne
S — Self is yielding to Christ
• — Interests are directed by Christ, resulting in harmony with God's plan

Which circle best represents your life?
Which circle would you like to have represent your life?

The following explains how you can receive Christ:

YOU CAN RECEIVE CHRIST RIGHT NOW BY FAITH THROUGH PRAYER

(Prayer is talking with God)

God knows your heart and is not so concerned with your words as He is with the attitude of your heart. The following is a suggested prayer:

"Lord Jesus, I need You. Thank You for dying on the cross for my sins. I open the door of my life and receive You as my Savior and Lord. Thank You for forgiving my sins and giving me eternal life. Take control of the throne of my life. Make me the kind of person You want me to be."

Does this prayer express the desire of your heart?

If it does, pray this prayer right now, and Christ will come into your life, as He promised.

How to Know That Christ Is in Your Life

Did you receive Christ into your life? According to His promise in Revelation 3:20, where is Christ right now in relation to you? Christ said that He would come into your life. Would He mislead you? On what authority do you know that God has answered your prayer? (The trustworthiness of God Himself and His Word.)

The Bible Promises Eternal Life to All Who Receive Christ

"And the witness is this, that God has given us eternal life, and this life is in His Son. He who has the Son has the life; he who does not have the Son of God does not have the life. These things I have written to you who believe in the name of the Son of God, in order that you may know that you have eternal life" (I John 5:11-13).

Thank God often that Christ is in your life and that He will never leave you (Hebrews 13:5). You can know on the basis of His promise that Christ lives in you and that you have eternal life, from the very moment you invite Him in. He will not deceive you.

An important reminder . . .

DO NOT DEPEND UPON FEELINGS

The promise of God's Word, the Bible — not our feelings — is our authority. The Christian lives by faith (trust) in the trustworthiness of God Himself and His Word. This train diagram illustrates the relationship between **fact** (God and His Word), **faith** (our trust in God and His Word), and **feeling** (the result of our faith and obedience) (John 14:21).

The train will run with or without the caboose. However, it would be useless to attempt to pull the train by the caboose. In the same way, we, as Christians, do not depend on feelings or emotions, but we place our faith (trust) in the trustworthiness of God and the promises of His Word.

NOW THAT YOU HAVE RECEIVED CHRIST

The moment that you received Christ by faith, as an act of the will, many things happened, including the following:

1. Christ came into your life (Revelation 3:20 and Colossians 1:27).
2. Your sins were forgiven (Colossians 1:14).
3. You became a child of God (John 1:12).
4. You received eternal life (John 5:24).
5. You began the great adventure for which God created you (John 10:10; II Corinthians 5:17 and I Thessalonians 5:18).

Can you think of anything more wonderful that could happen to you than receiving Christ? Would you like to thank God in prayer right now for what He has done for you? By thanking God, you demonstrate your faith. To enjoy your new life to the fullest . . .

SUGGESTIONS FOR CHRISTIAN GROWTH

Spiritual growth results from trusting Jesus Christ. "The righteous man shall live by faith" (Galatians 3:11). A life of faith will enable you to trust God increasingly with every detail of your life, and to practice the following:

G Go to God in prayer daily (John 15:7).

R Read God's Word daily (Acts 17:11)—begin with the Gospel of John.

O Obey God moment by moment (John 14:21).

W Witness for Christ by your life and words (Matthew 4:19; John 15:8).

T Trust God for every detail of your life (I Peter 5:7).

H Holy Spirit—allow Him to control and empower your daily life and witness (Galatians 5:16,17; Acts 1:8).

FELLOWSHIP IN A GOOD CHURCH

God's Word admonishes us not to forsake "the assembling of ourselves together. . ." (Hebrews 10:25). Several logs burn brightly together; but put one aside on the cold hearth and the fire goes out. So it is with your relationship to other Christians. If you do not belong to a church, do not wait to be invited. Take the initiative; call the pastor of a nearby church where Christ is honored and His Word is preached. Start this week, and make plans to attend regularly.

SPECIAL MATERIALS ARE AVAILABLE FOR CHRISTIAN GROWTH.

If you have come to know Christ personally through this presentation of the gospel, write for a free booklet especially written to assist you in your Christian growth.

A special Bible study series and an abundance of other helpful materials for Christian growth are also available. For additional information, please write Campus Crusade for Christ International, San Bernardino, CA 92414.

You will want to share this important discovery . . .